W9-CEL-715

'A marvellously astute, wry and affectionate account of France and the French – mercifully free of whimsy – and, moreover, written in pitch-perfect English prose. A delight.'
William Boyd

'Thorpe's memoir is not part of any herd. Nor does it belong in the fast-and-loose category of potboilers about swapping English life for continental idylls . . . It is erudite, firmly embedded in its own soil and yet evasive . . . Affectionate, appreciative and perceptive'
Observer

'Thorpe has dizzying range as well as style'
Daily Mail

'Powerful . . . Adam has all the gifts of novelist, correspondent, historian and poet'
Colin Greenwood

'In an altogether different class . . . Beautifully written, full of wisdom about the balance struck by humanity and the natural world between "ephemerality and permanence"'
The Tablet

'Erudite and beguiling'
The Times

'A marvellous evocation of the forgotten Languedoc'
Sigrid Rausing

'Deeply engaging . . . He has, in short, lived a life to which he was not born but which he has taken up and made his own, something many people dream about but few are able to emulate'
TLS

NOTES FROM
THE CÉVENNES

NOTES FROM
THE CÉVENNES

Half a Lifetime in Provincial France

Adam Thorpe

BLOOMSBURY CONTINUUM
LONDON · NEW YORK · OXFORD · NEW DELHI · SYDNEY

*In memory of my parents, who granted me a
love of two countries*

BLOOMSBURY CONTINUUM
Bloomsbury Publishing Plc
50 Bedford Square, London, WC1B 3DP, UK
29 Earlsfort Terrace, Dublin 2, Ireland

BLOOMSBURY, BLOOMSBURY CONTINUUM and the Diana logo are
trademarks of Bloomsbury Publishing Plc

First published in Great Britain 2018
Paperback, 2019

ISBN: HB: 978-1-4729-5129-8; PB: 978-1-4729-6631-5;
EPDF: 978-1-4729-5131-1; EPUB: 978-1-4729-5130-4

4 6 8 10 9 7 5 3

Typeset by Newgen KnowledgeWorks Pvt. Ltd., Chennai, India.
Printed and bound in Great Britain by CPI Group (UK) Ltd, Croydon CRO 4YY

To find out more about our authors and books visit www.bloomsbury.com
and sign up for our newsletters.

CONTENTS

CONTENTS

The urge to know was with me, and the ache. The smell of the soil, the gleam of the wet roads, the faded paint of shutters masking windows through which I should never look, the grey faces of houses whose doors I should never enter, were to me an ever-lasting reproach, a reminder of distance, of nationality . . . I should never be a Frenchman, never be one of them.

Daphne du Maurier, *The Scapegoat* (1959)

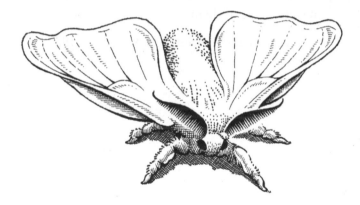

Gossamer Threads

We had been renting full-time in France for three years when we bought our house on the lower slopes of the Cévennes mountains: the last thrust of the Massif Central before the southern plain and the sea. An author's limited budget (one of the reasons for moving to France in the first place) meant that our reverie of an isolated *mas* or farmhouse with land around it soon dwindled to a rambling village house set against a hill, with a modest, unattached garden behind, sloping up in a series of terraces. At least the kids can walk to school, we told ourselves. Their route was a few minutes down a couple of rocky paths between drystone walls: we had read somewhere, in an article on human evolution, that unevenness underfoot stimulates the synapses, and with the lower path being particularly bouldery, we joked that this would turn them into geniuses.

'Your great-grandmother,' I told them, 'walked four miles a day to and from school in cold and rainy Derbyshire.' This was warm and relatively dry Languedoc. When it stormed, however, water from the sloping vineyard gushed furiously through a wall on the last stretch, adding to the challenge. Twenty-five years on, the way has recently been paved with shallow steps and cemented flat slabs, doing nothing for the neurones.

Our house is above the village proper. A cluster of largely medieval buildings on the side of a great dome-shaped hill thick with wild boars, our *quartier* feels like a separate hamlet, with its own name, threaded by rough-cobbled, sloping paths – *calades*, from the Occitan *calada* (Occitan being *la langue d'Oc*, giving rise to the region's name, Languedoc). The main *calade* passes right by our back door on its way up to the hamlet's green or *placette* – the beguiling suffix indicating its size, as a *cigarette* is a little *cigare*. This was dominated until a few years ago by the ruin of a medieval building, known as l'Hôpital. Not a hospital, but a refuge for the poorest or the insane. The lower village was destroyed in 1703 ('exterminated', in the no-nonsense words of the official command) by Louis XIV's dreaded dragoons of the green tunics, long black boots and five-foot sabres during the *guerres des religions*, as locals call them. Those that did the burning and demolishing were lodged in our sector, which is why it feels, in parts, like a medieval relic. There's still a warren of passageways where the old common well can be found, the bucket squeaking into a far-down splash.

Up until some 40 or 50 years ago, the wild limestone hill behind would have resembled the stepped tea or rice plantations of India or Vietnam, rising amphitheatrically with cultivated terraces called *bancèls* in Occitan, put to vegetables like onions, potatoes or leeks, planted with rows of vines, mulberries or olive trees (we are at the very limit of the latter's zone). The drystone support walls had to be continually repaired or the heavy rains of autumn and spring would eventually sweep the earth to the bottom, leaving only bare rock. Many *bancèls* have now vanished under bushes or secondary forest. You can see the evidence in the old photographs: a corrugation of thin terraces laboured over with mattock and two-pronged fork for all that the poor soil can give, helped by sheep manure carried in shoulder-yoked baskets up innumerable steps. There is a striking absence of mature trees in these vintage glimpses. The Cévennes were stripped of their timber in the eighteenth and nineteenth centuries – to be happily and heavily replanted in the twentieth with government aid.

The original walls are now half-tumbled among garrigue scrub, or lingering in stretches between pines, chestnut and spruce on the granitic part of our commune a couple of kilometres further north. Where the terraces are better preserved, in areas of the region where more springs bubble up in the aridity, back-to-earthers as well as locals have made beautiful gardens of them, green diadems draped on countless steep shelves. An old Berkshire saying, 'Ne'er come home wi'out stick or stone', has its Cévenol version in an enormous *clapàs* – a heap of collected stones – stretched among the slope's trees 50 yards above us. A bent-backed veteran warned me soon after our arrival that 'stones are all that grows in our soil'. And grow they do.

Dwarf holm oaks, patched with lichen, may thicken gloomily on the hill (I have grown fonder of them, of their plucky disdain of beauty as well as of cold or heat), but all of a sudden, in late April, the grey-green slopes turn psychedelic for a few weeks, splashed with brilliant orchids, wild garlic, flowering gorse, saxifrage, sage-leaved cistus, wild lavender and trailing honeysuckle, thyme, rosemary and countless other species that include my favourite, aphyllanthes, its tufts of pale electric-blue petals on frail grass-like stalks, blooming only in the day, appearing to wither to invisibility at dusk, then reviving in the morning. Their intense colour is fugitive, impossible to capture in a photograph: they come out a dull white. Small blue and yellow butterflies and grander ones like the scarce swallowtail flicker here and there as you step through the bristle of vegetation, breathing in the warm aromas that herald the imminent heat of cicada season.

At the top of our unprepossessing mount, lonely among the great boulders and sleeve-plucking junipers and thistly undergrowth, you can see the far-off Alps on a clear day, small and sharp as a shrew's lower teeth; Mont Ventoux fooling you with its snow-white summit of limestone; the great shadowy key-notes of Mont Aigoual and Mont Lozère to the north; the metallic gleam of the Mediterranean to the south. This peak is where I have stood when lacking inspiration, when my imagination feels valley-consigned, chained down, in need of re-urging.

The end house – part of a solid old *mas* – was occupied (and still is) by a family of Seventh Day Adventists, with numerous cousins living elsewhere in the area. The old pastor had just died when we arrived: Grégoire was his son. A bachelor in his thirties, he dressed in black trousers and jacket, sporting a pudding-basin haircut and carrying around with him a battered pocket Bible from which he would quote liberally and fervently when he passed us by the back door, sermonising on the Last Days and how Satan and his angels will rule over a desolate earth until burnt to ashes by God. A relative living in the nearest market town, possibly his aunt (it was never quite clear to me) and of an indefinable age, who dyed her loose hair a corresponding jet black and always wore the same long patterned dress, would trundle an old pram around in Stanley Spencer fashion: it held her shopping, mostly. She had an extraordinarily lugubrious way of speaking, almost a chant, a threnody of complaints with no punctuation. Her partner was a vague, beaming, round-faced presence whose own threaded suit, when he wasn't in a soiled vest, was pale brown and a size too large.

Very occasionally Grégoire would let rip with rock 'n' roll or New Orleans jazz at full blast from his bedroom's open windows: it would sound up and down the valley at odd times for a couple of hours. Locals would shrug and say, 'That's Grégoire for you. Letting it all out.' Eventually his married sister, born and bred in the *mas* and rarely leaving our hamlet even now ('Why should I? I don't like noise and I love my flowers and books!'), packed him off to a psychiatric hospital in town. He was like the ghost of old battles, of a lost fervour. An *illuminé*.

For this and for much else, despite the absence of grey skies and chalky mud, I felt that I had walked back into my recently published first novel, *Ulverton*, which concerns a downland village in Berkshire from the Civil War to 1988. The first chapter features a soldier called Gabby, returned to his homestead from Cromwell's conquest of Ireland after many years away, who finds that his wife has given him up for dead and married another. Gabby then disappears. When we were looking for a house to buy, a local in a neighbouring village told us how a farmer, glimpsed on his return from years of forced labour in Nazi Germany at the end of the last war, promptly vanished; his remarried wife and new husband were the main suspects, as they are in my novel, but the police were never involved.

'The family are still there,' he added, nodding at the house in question, which gave nothing away behind its shutters closed against the heat.

The novel is built up in chronological layers, each bleeding into the other. A palimpsest, where time's previous scribbles remain visible. Our house turned out to be the same, consisting of three formerly separate but now interleaved dwellings whose thick walls finally opened up to each other after yielding grudgingly to our *maçon*'s meaty drill. The drawings of Escher come to mind. The two parts at the rear are at the level of the back path, or what my Derbyshire father would have called a 'gennel'; these open into the spacious attic level of the main house, from which you have to descend to the first floor to reach the front door, which opens onto a curving flight of stone steps. Descending these to the front gennel, you pass the ancient wooden door of what was once a goat-house. A large square room with pine beams and a little ivy-clad window, an older neighbour remembers it being full of flies and the stink of goat dung, until the sanitary inspector was called. Areas of bare stone or flaking *crépi* (rough-cast lime render) gave the house a certain scuffed look that we've not touched.

Overlaid levels of historical periods, from Gallo-Roman on the ground floor to eighteenth century under the roof, teased us with clues. For instance, the small entrance hall on the first floor was once the kitchen. A great oak beam, a foot across, strengthened in the middle by slightly less ancient iron straps, displays a formidable hook, sturdy enough to take a whole pig, wild or domestic. A shallow sink survives, chiselled out of stone, lacking only a water pitcher and basin. The centuries-old floor, tiled in thick terracotta, slopes down towards the outside door for easy sluicing: there is a small wooden trap set into the tiles, through which our elderly neighbour remembers, as a boy, 'pouring the grapes trampled into a mush by my bare feet: there was this big wooden vat in the cellar below, directly below the trap'. This cellar, like its larger companion, is actually at ground level, and was reserved for farm-produce such as olives or wine, as the other was used for livestock, in the way of the traditional housebarn familiar from prehistoric times on. Both *caves* are still earth-floored. 'We did it all for free,' my neighbour continued. 'It was only enough wine for the family itself. Their vineyard went down to the road, back then . . .'

The vines were replaced, back in the 1960s, by an uncompromising block of a house and the corrugated roof of its builder's yard. But I say nothing, as the notoriously volatile hunter who owns it is still very much of the present. And the present slips away like a fish. A home is not only an archaeological strata of long-lost times, of course, but (in our case) a place for family, a living continuum where personal memories are triggered by dusty toys, dried-up poster-paints, a painted clay lump in the bottom of a box.

The sellers were equally typical of the region: Parisian *néoruraux* who had made ceramic wall-tiles in the main *cave* until impoverishment turned them into social workers. Not so different from ourselves: I was fashioning novels and poems instead of tiles, and Jo soon became a teacher. Their cobalt-blue efforts still grace our unimproved bathroom, set back into the hill and windowless. To reach the second floor you have a choice of staircases: one, the original spine of the house in lime mortar and oakwood, lies towards the back; the other angles up from the entrance hall, fashioned in chestnut by the village carpenter. The second floor was once the attic or *magnanerie* under the eaves, where silkworms munched on mulberry leaves spread over wickerwork trays rising in tiers: a profitable home industry before artificial fibres made it redundant after the war. Soon after we arrived, I was shown such an attic, the trays or 'beds' still intact, in a house that was for sale in the village: perhaps the last glimpse of a practice dating from the thirteenth century. The impoverished Cévennes, once notorious for their sickly and undernourished population, produced France's favourite luxury item thanks to the white (not the black) mulberry, nicknamed *l'arbre d'or* or 'tree of gold'. Fiercely pollarded to resemble a child's pipe-cleaner sculpture, they produced large and juicy leaves. Cévenol silk was regarded as 'perhaps the finest in the world', even by British commentators.[1] Meanwhile, right up to the last war, many *paysans* were so poor they went about in bare feet to avoid wearing out their clogs, which they hung on string around their necks until they reached town, donning them for market or church and slipping them off for the path home. Wasting something was unknown, money hardly seen and everything was reused, like the flattened tin colander serving as an animal flap on our back cellar's door.

In April, our children would bring back silkworm eggs from school as part of an annual project. In the old days, these were wrapped in cloth sachets and tucked between the warm breasts or thighs of the woman of the house, despite posters warning *Ne faites jamais l'incubation dans le corsage* (Never use a bodice for incubation). Tiny black worms appeared and, instantly gorging on fresh mulberry leaves, grew fat

[1]Ure, Andrew, *The Philosophy of Manufactures: Or, An Exposition of the Scientific, Moral, and Commercial Economy of the Factory System of Great Britain* (London: C. Knight, 1835), p. 251.

and translucently white, like a resplendently helmeted maggot, the heart beating visibly in the tail. At one point, we had around 80 tiny jaws working through the daily supply from the three old mulberries that still grace our terraced garden, their forms gnarled and swollen by centuries of pollarding. The sound is like the rustle of rain in a wood. Within weeks the worms had climbed into the twig forest we had artfully arranged on the trays and begun to spin a mist of gossamer threads around them. These thickened and hardened into cocoons, within which the chrysalid brooded. In the old days, we'd have hung them like onion strings until the *pesage* or weighing day on the square, when the silk factory took over. Then the workers – always women – killed the pupa inside by dipping the cocoon in boiling water and releasing the loosened thread onto its bobbin; silk-workers' fingers were red and swollen from being effectively parboiled day after day in the spinning mill. It took two thousand cocoons to make one silk dress.

The very last mill in the Cévennes, with its own orchard of mulberries, is still active at the entrance to our village, more a hopeful revival than a continuity, as the original *filature* lies long and hollow-windowed along the high street. We got as far as pinching loose thread from the cocoons and rolling a rougher version between our fingers.

It was exciting, anyway, to watch the moths hatch, their useless wings dusted as if with chalk, the cocoons left dangling like old skin. Finding their mate, the cycle began again. New eggs, fresh worms. What was the original point of it all, before a Chinese princess discovered the properties of silk? It seems an existential question. Nature gives point to herself. We would have kept it going for ages, this miraculous sequence, if the second year's batch of eggs overwintering in the fridge hadn't turned yellow following a power cut. It was a shame, a trivial echo of the various calamities – disease, hard frosts, war, anti-Huguenot oppression, competition from China – that a thriving regional industry, producing hundreds of thousands of pounds of silk at its height in the nineteenth century, barely survived each time. The house had seemed to have rediscovered its old pulse, its former pungencies of mulberry leaf and worm, but it was an educational game, not a matter of life or starvation.

A sepia postcard of our village square, entitled *Scènes Cévenoles*, shows the *pesage officiel des cocons* around the turn of the nineteenth century: bloated sacks lying on wooden tables, bullocks and carts in the background, men in droopy moustaches drawing up their sleeves or self-importantly striding about while the women – then, as now, running the business side of each household – lean on the stone parapet (identical today) and await the verdict of the scales. The private Harvest ready to be sold to the silk factory. This was money, spun from a delicate, intense labour of around five weeks.

The square's magnificent mulberry visible in the photo to one side, much pollarded and knobbed by calluses, its hefty long arms of branches stripped of every juicy leaf, still survives in much diminished form, its rotted-out hollow in the middle first filled with concrete in the 1960s. This tree nearly killed me.

One morning after an arts festival, helping to clear up, I was releasing a rope wrapped around one of the surviving branches when my vision was filled by an enormous grey lump falling slowly towards me, like a meteorite in a low-budget film. I had sufficient microseconds, elongated by shock, to lift my arm and turn my head away. The concrete boulder rolled over my elbow joint and carried on down to my skull. Incredibly, as the world jarred, I had time to think how ridiculous this all was. What a way to go!

Lying on the ground next to my attacker, I saw the village café sideways on, disgorging people who, having witnessed the accident, immediately began to run towards me down the side of my vision, as in the Larkin poem 'Days', in which the priest and the doctor in their long coats come 'running over the fields'. They were carrying bandages and France's salvatory antiseptic for all occasions, *Betadine*, whose bright red colour makes any wound look twice as dramatic. I heard a friend cry through the gathering fog, '*Ah ʒut, il y a un trou* [Oh dear, there's a hole]!' Fortunately this note of horror (I imagined she could see the brain) was referring to my ear: according to the village doctor, to whose tiny *cabinet* I was taken immediately, his massive German Shepherd shoved apologetically off the examination couch, my ear had saved my life with its rubbery structure, as just behind it lay the most vulnerable part of the skull, known by assassins with stiletto knives.

The hole referred to was in the ear flap, so I was doubly lucky. If I had been struck anywhere else on the head, he breezily explained, my skull would have cracked like a coconut.

Afterwards I was told that the concrete had seemed to bounce off my head, just missing my daughter, then four years old. Paul, the mayor at the time, who had been responsible for patching up the tree all those years before, bought me a beer in the café (owned and run for generations by his wife Lydie's family) and was ruefully apologetic. 'We wanted to save that tree, it's part of our cultural heritage, but we should have checked it out.' Lydie, behind the bar, claimed she'd told him it was loose, like an old filling. It was clearly ready to fall at any moment. My fiddling with the rope had possibly saved someone else – one of the children gathered around the trunk during a future arts festival, for instance – from having their head bashed in.

The tree still flourishes, with a serious pillar of fresh concrete shoring it up, but I often reflect on how close I came to becoming a fatality, however oblique, of the Cévenol silk industry.

Which is mostly historical, although fireflies of its presence still glow: once, in the neighbouring mountain village, sitting near me on the bench, a man in his nineties was gazing on the famously long high street when the midday bell tolled. He turned to me and said: '*Vous savez*, at this time of the day, before the war, you'd have a sudden flood. All the women from the silk factory pouring down here in their cardigans and dresses and wooden *sabots* thundering on the cobbles. Hundreds of them. Wall to wall, shoulder to shoulder. A tidal wave. Flooding down here, laughing and shouting. Happy, because they're off to lunch!'

The former *magnanerie* under our roof, once with a hearth or stove in every corner to keep the temperature steady for the worms whatever the exigencies of the weather whistling outside, is now our kitchen, dining-room and sitting-room set out in an L-shape. Nothing remains of that peasant struggle to keep a balance between warmth and ventilation, nor of that extreme sensitivity to smell which might indicate something subtly awry: the air had to smell green and fresh, despite the billows of smoke, and thyme or lavender would be spread for sweetness.

So much peasant expertise and knowledge, mostly lost.

The sprawl of rooms on several levels still bewilders our occasional guests, as do the four staircases. In an understandable if risky move, the *néoruraux* had lifted away the lowest, front part of the roof to make an outdoor balcony, with a view extending almost to the Mediterranean, her waters bouncing the light back up in a blanched glow along the horizon. It isn't quite as breathtaking as the scope of the hill's summit behind us, but the view wooed us then, and can still surprise us now; never the same, the semicircle of distance is dominated by a sky that can yield marvels of cloudscapes and Turneresque effects, even at night, when a widescreen starriness takes over. To the west, the panorama includes the oak-draped crags – identical cones if viewed from each end, long high bluffs from the side, like mesas – that are the village emblem, happily forming its initial letter 'M' and nicknamed 'the twins', 'the camel' or, more graphically, 'the tits'. To the east, the walls and tower of a ruined thirteenth-century chateau perch like a child's drawing on a dome-shaped hill, always catching the last of the sun like a gilded knob on a pot lid. The castle was built by Blanche of Castile as an outlying garrison post against the Cathars. She visited it once on her white horse, so they say. Unlike the *hôpital*, it is protected as a heritage site.

Buzzards and kestrels float the currents and, at exactly our eye level, swifts and swallows swoop and screech twice a year on their way up or down from Africa. Recently we saw a dozen vultures flap their lazy way overhead, and we occasionally struggle with the binoculars as a huge, glider-winged golden eagle soars above us. Every spring, a scops owl down in the valley begins its endless night beeping, as if the impending heat is reversing towards us.

This view, and the affordable price, blinded us to the house's dilapidation, made worse by those previous bungling efforts at improvement. The broad spreads of roof, handsomely laid to terracotta *tuiles romaines*, had appeared intact, guilelessly confirmed by the sellers. At the first rainstorm, the sitting-room was an assault course of pots, pans and pails. The balcony regularly leaked rain into my study, scoring the plaster after a serious storm: it was to take twenty-odd years and a chunk of our accumulated savings to solve this. Water came in under the back door and spread patiently into the back room. The one overtly professional job done by the former owners was the stark white ceramic tiling of the entire first floor, the kind of surface you find in hospital operating rooms. We'd see to the leaks first, the tiles second – when finances permitted.

Our crumbly façade faces straight onto the front gennel, or *calade*, which snakes up and back on itself, eventually to greet the rear door some two storeys higher. It becomes a bubbling stream during a storm. The house is not approachable by car, only by mule, bike or on foot. With our three small kids often playing outside, having the fields and woods as their playground, this was a point in its favour. Although the house does not have any garden immediately around it, there was something about us not standing in our own penumbra of territorial ownership that was pleasing.

A few stone steps the other side of the *calade* and you're in the patch that is currently ours. Climbing up the steep hillside in a wide and narrowing strip, it consists of six *bancèls* once set to potatoes and onions and now to flowers, grass, a pond, and too many trees. Mending or, in some cases, re-establishing the drystone walls has become an obsessive hobby, the stones soldered only by a mixture of instinct and calculation. The previous owners were proud of their evergreen sapling: in the nearly three decades we've been here, this cedar of Lebanon's ambition to cast all three lower terraces into shade has made serious headway.

Its main competitor is a huge *micocoulier*, or hackberry (*Celtis occidentalis*), known locally as a *forquièr* from its use in the nearby production of three-pronged hay forks teased out of carefully trained branches. Since it is deciduous yet drought-resistant, you find it gracing the avenues of every southern French town, yet it is much less famous than the plane tree. Its tiny berries consist mainly of the stone, but the fleshy rind is tasty, reminiscent of juniper berry and gorged on by birds. Locals dismiss the fruit as inedible, despite it being a forage food for half a million years, so I nibble on the windfalls, feeling eccentric. I may, however, be supping on the 'delicious' lotus in the *Odyssey* and in Herodotus's *Histories* and, by extension, on the 'enchanted' fruits in Tennyson's 'The Lotos-Eaters' ('whoso did receive of them, / And taste, to him the gushing of the wave / Far far away did seem to mourn and rave . . .'). The hackberry is a serious candidate for the original lotus: significantly, perhaps, it is part of the cannabis family.

Small life goes on through the eruptions of history: the plaster-moulded fireplace in my study was signed by the owner in 1789. This was a common practice, I was told, a hidden mark of proprietorship. It was a chance discovery: gently peeling the flaking cream distemper back to the original sky-blue limewash, the pencilled strokes appeared in a bare patch. I was told that, in the old days, the entire room – walls, chimney-piece, window-frames – would have been painted in this blue, said to be off-putting to flies and mosquitoes and now unreproducible. It's a beautiful colour, with the subtly varying hues of limewash, but it's hard to imagine the room in its former all-over glory. Like an aquarium, perhaps.

A few inches below the ceiling, visible under the peeling distemper, a thick brown line frames the blue, as roughly done as the Roman equivalent in Pompeii or, much closer to home, on unearthed fragments of burnt-out villas in Nîmes. There is a spiritedness in such roughness, almost an expressionism. Perhaps that's why facsimiles and reproductions of past times look so fake: we paint and do up our houses as members of the machine age. I prefer the unsentimental simplicity evoked by Seamus Heaney in 'Lightenings', with home condensed to 'A latch, a door-bar, forged tongs and a grate'.

The building bears scars, too. The back door's ancient stone arch, made up of two huge and curving slabs, has an array of long shallow cuts on its inner edge, like a crude sculptural depiction of tucked-in folds. A villager demonstrated to me how these were made, producing an Opinel knife from his pocket and sharpening it in one of the grooves. What could be more convenient than having, just over your head as you pass in and out, a giant whetstone for your myriad tools? On the single slab of front-door sill, smoother to the touch, there are similar marks. Dip the blade into water, bend down, undull its edge, and you're ready for the day.

Rather as with our own skin, not all the marks suffered by the house are traces of the practical, or of mere accidents, or of age. Some are the equivalent of tattoos. On the door of one of our cellars facing the front *calade*, I noticed a heart had been carefully carved. There are two large letters filling it, an A and an M, separated by a large dot. The lettering is old-fashioned and looks eighteenth century or earlier, the 'A' with a cross stroke like a bent branch. Both glyphs have serifs, or feet, on the end of each outer stroke. It's as if one of my favourite writer-artists has paid the house a visit with his burin: David Jones – poet, painter and calligrapher, whose lettering was modelled on Roman inscriptions – *woʒ here*.

I find another on a beam in the kitchen: it is larger and wilder, without the love-heart, while its 'A' glyph is turned into a sort of tent, with an additional vertical in the middle and with no cross stroke. A semicircle tops the apex like a setting sun. It resembles a carpenter's mark more than anything, or perhaps a secret symbol between lovers, or between local rebels during the Camisard Wars. At any rate, someone in this house was passionate about someone else whose initials were A and M, and who, like Orlando in *As You Like It* pinning his heart to trees, could not contain the message. He had to shout it from the beams and doors.

Run, run, Orlando; carve on every tree,
The fair, the chaste, and unexpressive she.

On the other hand, it's possible that these are the initial letters of the couple, brought together in love. An Angel Clare enfolded with a Tess.

I examine other wooden surfaces for evidence, starting of course with the remaining doors, inside and outside. Broad unframed slabs of planked oak, with hand-wrought nails, heart-shaped drop-handles smoothed by centuries of touch, and opening to the sharply individual clunk of a latch, they are likely to be centuries old.

The hinges on these doors are the original strap hinges: long flat bars of iron stretching over half of the door's width, hand-forged and crudely beautiful. In a classic design known as 'Gothic', because of their popularity during the Middle Ages, the ends of each hinge form a curly C like a flower or an open mouth. Our carpenter reckoned there was a central tongue or petal that had been chiselled off during the Revolution, as ours could have been mistaken for the classic fleur-de-lys type – one central petal and two outer petals curling back rather than (as ours do) forward. The fleur-de-lys, being a royal symbol, was mutilated in this way out of either republican fervour or fearful caution, leaving only the two outer petals. You find similarly mutilated fleur-de-lys on antique items as varied as brass sword-guards or the decorative metalwork of a dresser.

It is another eerie gust from the Revolution, and with his leather gauntlet protecting the stumps of three fingers and a thumb long ago removed by an encounter with a circular saw, our carpenter resembles an old revolutionary himself. He told us that the penalty for retaining anything royal in your house could be death. 'Once,' he went on, 'I was asked to work on a small church. I opened a forgotten, half-broken little shutter high up in the wall, covered in cobwebs. And there were two untouched fleur-de-lys hinges, perfectly intact. *Mon dieu*, the only ones I've ever seen! I don't suppose anyone had opened that shutter for centuries, from the look of it.'

I have examined all our old hinges, including those squeaking on our most ancient and dilapidated shutters. There are definite signs of mutilation and not one central petal. On the other hand, they may simply be the 'Gothic' type, roughly wrought by a rural blacksmith – which is less dramatic as a notion but equally resonant of the past.

There are no more love tokens. I am reasonably sure that, on first arriving, I found several in that first freshness of exploration. But they seem to have flown. All that's left here and there on the tall oaken pages, apart from mysterious burn-marks like black thumbprints, are faint scribbles, circles, lines and tallies scratched with a sharp implement, as if a child or an apprentice has, at various moments over the last centuries, idly whiled away a dull moment. Meagre evidence of complex lives, but a lot better than a new door.

2

The Poppet

Sometimes the overlaid periods are startling. The cellar at the back a few steps below ground level, and including a fireplace, bread-oven and bricked-up window, is effectively an intact medieval cottage, with a lightless room beyond boasting two more blocked-up windows. As I scraped away the accumulated humus, turning up the rusty tip of a lance and a little glazed jug, the earth floor turned into stone flags – a real proof of ancientness in this area, earlier than terracotta tiles – while the cellar's own door is a Cubist abstract of repairs. It was here, on the bread-oven's upper slab in among the straw and goat-pellets, that I found the legless, naked torso of a svelte 1950s doll, its nipples, navel and temples pierced by tiny nails. I guessed immediately that it was a witchcraft 'poppet', its lids closing creepily over sparkly blue eyes. It still lies where I found it all those years ago; although the Museum of Witchcraft at Boscastle in Cornwall fancy a photograph for their poppet collection, I am sufficiently superstitious to keep on postponing the shoot.

Even at the time of the find, the experience of a few months of village life was sufficient to convince me that this was the genuine folk-magic article, probably designed to cause pain rather than relief. When Madame Mourier, our immediate neighbour in our first years, told me that she had once housed her mule in the same rented cellar, I began to wonder if the poppet was her doing. Even to the most lackadaisical witchfinder general, she fitted the bill: an old, sinewy *paysanne* who dressed in the same classic blue apron coat and printed skirt whatever the season, she had a curious habit of glowering in your direction until you caught her eye, whereupon she would snap into a shy smile. One of her many grown-up children had *troubles mentaux*, if more extreme than Grégoire's. Bruno would stand mute and mysterious on the *calade* much of the day; unearthly screams from the dark kitchen would indicate that he was back inside, still mute, being ticked off by his mum. My children preferred to take the back gennel on their way to school, despite my lectures on neighbourliness.

Evidence that Madame Mourier wasn't spinning me a yarn came not only in the form of a hand-forged billhook and other tools, half-concealed under straw in the lightless cellar's stone trough, and a crooked home-made ladder that puffed into sawdust when I lifted it, but hanging pieces of harness and a vet's bill, dated 1952, mice-nibbled but legible, made out to her late husband. The harness was in chunky, sharp-smelling leather and as complete as a short poem: cheekpieces, blinkers, hand-forged bit buckle, browband, noseband, winkerstay buckle and throat lash. A crupper or *culeron* or, in Occitan, a *socoa*, dangled from a beam, the stitched leather stiff with age but still serviceable.

Among other parts, including leather tugs with carved billets like a duffle coat's toggles for looping over the shafts of a cart (Oc *suefra*), I uncovered what I thought was the yoke stock nearby, crudely fashioned from a single thick and unbarked branch, its non-matching, rusty iron traces intact enough to be pulled, tinkling percussively. How familiar that sound must have been to her! She smiled more uncertainly when I showed her these, as if embarrassed by the evidence of her gruelling former life, by the fact that I should have lifted it back into daylight.

Years later I took the harness to Dédé, who runs a local stables and comes from the Camargue. He scoffed at the yoke idea. It was a primitive swingletree – the crossbar to which the traces are attached and which makes pulling steadier and less sore on the shoulders for the animal. 'The traces are made up of chains that were just lying about. That's how it was in the old days, when most people round here were really poor. You improvised.' He explained how carts had runners rather than wheels. 'Sliding's easier. You put your sacks of potatoes, or stones, dung, timber, hay or whatever on the knocked-together *traîneau*, and away you went.' He laid out the swingle's traces and picked up the branch they were crudely attached to. 'They hooked whatever they wanted onto this. But this really is *n'importe quoi*.' There was a proper swingle tree, a semicircle of iron tubing bubbled with rust, hanging on the side of the barn. 'Here, have it,' he said, handing its surprising weight over. I protested, but he took no notice and stopped by an anvil near the hedge. 'And here's a mule's shoe to go with it. You see? Much narrower in shape than a horse's, turned over at either end to stop it sliding in the mud. Mules,' he added, pointing to two of his own in the field, 'are much more intelligent than horses. They stop and reflect. They'll be obstinate, but only with a stranger. They were everywhere in the old times. They'll come back again, one day.'

I returned with a treasure, not only of time-corroded harness and equipment, but of exquisite knowledge.

It seems strange that Madame Mourier should have left such stuff behind in her rented cellar, but clearly it was already superfluous and unsellable in the convulsion of technological and social change that put paid, within a few years in the West, to a millennial practice, to the brays and snorts of draft animals and to so much else. Now, along with my garden-excavated, rust-ravaged sheep or goat bells and old keys – enough to unlock a castle – the various found items hang silently in my study, a decorative trope which a friend and artist colleague brought up on a farm by *paysan* parents finds horribly bourgeois.

'No,' I insisted, 'it's not decorative, Hubert, it's historical. I'm a curator of time.'

It sounded better in French.

I knew all about Madame Mourier's late husband from his brother, Albert. On my first outing to the village bakery, a sinewy old man had emerged from his potato patch and disguised his curiosity with an affable greeting. Affable greetings were in short supply in the village, but on telling him where I lived, his tone changed. 'Then you live next door to my sister-in-law,' he growled, with a dramatic stare.

'Oh, that's nice,' I said.

'No, no,' he went on, 'she's evil!'

Evil?

'She killed my brother!'

I thought he was joking, but he made me follow him into his dark barn, littered with old iron-hooped wine casks. Madame Mourier had, he claimed, picked up a kitchen knife and tried to stab his brother with it, forcing the poor man to sleep out in the fields for days, weeping all the while. The mime that accompanied this account was energetic: I'm tempted to call it a dance.

Albert, my new friend, had been a prisoner for seven years in Germany, forced to toil in the fields on starvation rations; his long and arduous return (mostly on foot) ended with him raising a hand to a strange young man in the outlying vineyards. It was his brother, unrecognisably grown up. 'This was her husband, the brother she killed!' yelled Albert as I expressed astonishment. He was dancing again from foot to foot against the bright sun blazing in the doorway.

'But she didn't actually kill him,' I ventured, dreading the idea of living next door to a murderess.

Albert nodded slowly. 'She killed him, for certain. He was driven out of the house and he died from grief.'

I breathed a sigh of relief. What had provoked her to this act?

'My brother worked hard in the fields,' Albert said, gripping my forearm as if to feel the evidence of a life spent quite otherwise. 'Who can blame him if he got thirsty now and again?' In other words, I thought, nodding concernedly, the man was a boozer. Madame Mourier had already told me how she would carry water twice a day for their potatoes in two yoked buckets over her shoulders, all the way up from her well to what was now our steep-sloped garden full of effeminate blooms. Eight children, a mule, an alcoholic husband and dry, stony land to till. No car, of course, so families were stuck with each other, several to a room, the oldest generation hanging on with them, even when incontinent or senile. Very little passing traffic: the village was never on a trade route. Of course she had to crack now and again.

I considered a further possibility: that, although there was little resemblance between the tiny blonde bombshell of a poppet and Madame Mourier, she or her family were the intended victim. This idea occurred to me after her daughter-in-law, Jocelyne, gave us the story behind Bruno's speechlessness.

One Sunday, the entire Mourier family had sat down to lunch, happily chatting, when the eldest son said he had to go upstairs to his childhood bedroom to fetch something. 'To fetch something,' Jocelyne repeated, 'that's all he said.' A few minutes later, an explosion rocked the tiny house: the son's shotgun. Bruno – always 'over-sensitive', Jocelyne explained (a serious charge in these Calvinist hills) – was the first to reach the top room. Bruno had not spoken a word in the three years since. Jocelyne added that, having been assigned (in her professional capacity as a *femme de ménage*) to clean up the room with the help of several bottles of *eau de Javel* and a scrubbing brush, she retrieved an eyeball from under the bed. I asked her what had driven her brother-in-law to do such a thing. 'He became a bit depressive,' she said, 'after his father had passed away. But that's all. Inexplicable!'

Madame Mourier would sometimes refer, in her elusive way, to the 'terrible thing' that had turned her poor Bruno's mind. But she was tough. During the harsh winters, like most Cévenols, she had descended to the village and broken thick ice in the fountain that served as a washing-place, before running water was introduced in the 1960s. When, soon after our arrival, she encouraged the stove one morning with a spurt of oil and set her apron coat alight, running ablaze round and round the table, a moaning Bruno in hot pursuit, she weathered her legs' serious burns for weeks with barely a groan. In her latter years she would stand for ages on the road below in that unchanging blue outfit, even in a freezing wind. To think how that entire generation, intimate with the final years of a pre-industrial agriculture, has now gone into the dark: it makes me feel choked with a diffuse and helpless grief. I took her for granted, I suppose. As I did all her English companions-in-time, whom I would chat with for hours in dim downland pubs some 40 years back.

She did, however, have a soft spot for cats, and would adopt strays. Their brief arcadia spent purring around her legs would always end in the same way, beside the same plastic feeding bowl. She showed me a stiff, stone-cold victim one morning, shaking a vengeful fist at the 1960s house beyond her chicken-wire hen coop through what in anyone else would have been tears. Although I reckoned the house's owner, the hunter famous for his temper, might not think twice about poisoning cats, I refrained from mentioning my chief suspect. The feeding bowl, she hissed, was from her own kitchen. What a cheek! And they've even used my late husband's rat poison!

Bruno, of course, kept a discreet silence, taut and lean in the shadows. He disappeared into a psychiatric hospital some years before Madame Mourier's death around 15 years back. The tiny, pimple-sized nails in the poppet are now oxidised green and ready to crumble off. But not yet, not quite. It still lies there on the old bread-oven in the cellar, demanding respect, and I for one am happy to grant it.

3

Coming Into Shot

'This is really post-modernist,' Jo observed, not knowing whether the enamel sign on the high street (ALIMENTATION) was true or false. Within a fortnight of our arrival in the village, a film crew had moved in. This had nothing to do with us, but it felt as though it did: the last chapter of *Ulverton*, now lately published (the novel's title was the name of my imaginary Berkshire village), was in the form of a TV documentary script. The old enamel *panneaux* on the square, indicating the direction to neighbouring villages and the nearest towns, were swapped for identical types (white, with blue edging) featuring entirely invented names. Having barely worked out our bearings in a pre-GPS age, we found this confusing.

The village at that time had an *épicerie* near the *boulangerie*, but the production company decided it wasn't authentic enough and bought (or fashioned) the rustier, antique-looking plaque announcing Groceries, fixed it to a building on the high street that had once been a shop, and hung net curtains in the windows. The café sprouted a red Tabac sign – the elongated lozenge type known as the '*carrotte du tabac*' – while, a few doors up, the homely local restaurant had its pleasant cream façade painted a horrible brown. This, I was told, was to 'knock it back' for lighting purposes as much as to give it an older look, despite the present-day setting of the TV film that all this disruption was serving. Amazingly, both the fake sign, the Tabac 'carrot' and the horrible brown have survived to this day. What is true, what is false? Or, as a distinguished writer friend put it to me recently: 'Do we write our novels, or do our novels write us?'

To confuse things further, much of the action took place in the village school, genuinely threatened with the closure of one of its classes. The TV film's main thrust was the closure of the entire school from lack of numbers. To save it, a grandmother in her seventies (played by a veteran star, I was told – *'elle est assez connue'*) enrols at the beginning of the year and nothing in French law can prevent her being accepted. Thus she squeezes behind the miniature desk and, with her occasional remarks, annoys the stiff-backed male teacher and makes her classmates laugh. Some of my sons' new friends had to attend simulated lessons and pretend to play in the little playground, several even being given lines. Admittedly our school was housed (until very recently) in the absolute essence of what one imagines a nineteenth-century village *école* should look like, a standard slice of the north in the south, complete with a redundant *Filles* and *Garçons* rendered in stone above the two entrances.

I already felt a bit unreal, anyway, in our new life, after three years renting in an isolated oxbow, but now

I would never quite know, wandering down to buy supplies or to deliver the kids to school, whether what I was watching was authentic live action or entirely sham. I arrived in the *place* one day to see the old tractor used in village fêtes trundling very slowly and aimlessly from one side of the square to the other, which seemed strange until I was told that they were filming from one corner: they didn't mind people coming into shot as long as we avoided waving or looking self-conscious. On no account were we to act. A lot of green bamboos in pots had been placed on the steep and winding approach to hide an admittedly ugly concrete wall supporting one end of the square. Unfortunately, these didn't stay.

Extras were recruited at pocket-money rates for a scene in the neighbouring town, where the fictional local officials were up in arms about the new pupil. I thought of volunteering, but chickened out, terrified I'd be asked to speak, so revealing my foreignness. A new friend, Jacques, who still lives in an old and very narrow house at the bottom of the path to school, was a seasoned actor who had begun in the Comédie Française and worked under the distinguished director Marcel Maréchal; he had a scene all to himself, playing a waiter in town. (The following year and for many years subsequently, he would star in a dramatised version of *Ulverton* that we would occasionally tour, in settings as varied as a Parisian theatre-café and along a three-mile walking route in the mountains.) I glimpsed the star, the well-known actress in her sixties: she came across in the eventual film as a sweet old dear who adored kids, but in reality she was a nightmare to work with and loathed children – as was gleefully reported by our own.

Many years later, I drove the writer Michel Jeury (who lived nearby) to the filming of one of his best-known novels, a grim Resistance tale set in the Second World War. Jeury, the son of peasants himself, writes in the popular vein of rural novels of peasant life, as if Thomas Hardy's seam has continued to be worked by novelists in a country where industrialisation arrived much later, and where Stella Gibbons's devastating rural satire, *Cold Comfort Farm*, was never emulated. The large and remote village up in the high Cévennes, with a river rushing through it under a series of ancient bridges, hardly had to be altered, I was told – 'the inhabitants included,' added one of the crew. Only the Crédit Agricole sign was hidden behind a rectangle of wood. Actors in 1940s dress dotted the lanes, and any car dating after 1945 was parked out of sight.

We were allowed (writer's privilege) to sit in a classroom in the school, where an important scene was to be filmed, and which had been suitably converted with minute attention to detail. It was like sitting in the opening pages of *Madame Bovary*, which begins: 'We were in study-hour, when the Headmaster entered . . .' It also felt very like the classrooms of my childhood: a metal stove with an iron flue; inkwells in the scarred wooden bench-desks, blackboards with chalk on string, and oilcloth posters of the world (which included, in this mocked-up version, a large one of the Third Reich).

The hired extras were as immaculately period as the setting: ears sticking out of clipped hair, shirt-smocks, obedience. We were there two hours, the camera and sound-boom safely in front of us: the scene involved a Gestapo officer and a well-dressed woman arriving by car and entering the building. The car was a black Maybach, gorgeously polished and throbbing through the window as it delivered its visitors.

I can honestly say that there were moments when I faded out of my own time and into that of my parents. My mind was bamboozled. I could, I thought, have so easily been there. I was born in Paris some 11 years after the end of the war. Barely enough to register a change in décor. Things moved more slowly then. The road signs were the enamel Michelin type embedded in concrete that you only find these days in places like the Ile d'Ouessant, mistily brooding some 20 kilometres off the Brittany coast. Many of the cars themselves would have been of pre-war vintage. My father drove a 1938 Type 57 Bugatti, bought (among other reasons) because it was cheaper than any new vehicle. I cut my lip on it when he braked too hard on a cobbled Paris street and I was thrown forward onto the back of the leather seat in front – a distressing incident which became one of my earliest and most vivid memories.

So here I was, in a rural wartime French classroom, finding it almost more familiar than my genuine memories of being schooled in England. And it was all fake. What made it more real, perhaps, was that it was cold. The stove didn't function, of course, and the mountain air was fresh. Even wiry Michel suffered, and he was not a young man. The smells were of old wooden floorboards, beeswax and must. I was falling for the teacher, a slim young woman in a fetching patterned dress and bobbed hair. *Please, miss . . .*

When eventually we watched the TV film shot in our village, we were amazed by the beauty of the landscape shots and the falsity of everything else. The dialogue was wooden, the situation unbelievable, the overall mood sentimental. Nothing looked quite like the village itself, although the place was the same. It was disconcerting. The film had decent reviews and was repeated.

We recently fished out the video and got our dusty machine to work. The local children who'd impressed us and themselves in the school scenes are now adults, many with families of their own. The electricity pylons that scarred the village, but which we barely noticed, have now been dismantled. The big, bare hill behind, uninterruptedly green with trees, is now dotted with new houses. A travelling shot shows the heroine entering the village, passing a long green verge full of flowers; this has just been replaced by a massive breezeblock wall, topped by wire like something out of a sci-fi detention camp: the new owners of the roadside property, originally from a northern suburb, proud owners of a black Mitsubishi pick-up truck, have to keep their two big dogs from straying, it was explained by their tactful neighbour, a beekeeper.

It all seems a long time ago, preserved in the film as under glass. The lightweight entertainment has become a document. After all, the final 'contemporary' chapter in *Ulverton*, taking place in 1988, is also now a generation back. Like the TV film it so eerily anticipated, it has become almost historical.

4

Wartime Shrines

The other day I met Elie, the old one-eyed goatherd, in an unexpected place: our local organic food co-operative. He was shovelling kilos of basmati rice into paper bags, and made a joke about the British Empire. He and his sister have a herd of about 20 goats, and live together in the farmhouse they were born in before the war – one of the last in our area to have the feel of a real farm: chained-up dog, metal and plastic debris, ramshackle fencing, heaps of straw and a pungent smell of animals.

I've had many conversations with Elie, an autodidact whose ultimate dream is to live in Iceland. He writes poems in English, claiming he has never learnt the language but that they come to him in reverie. After much searching in an outhouse, he found a stained brown envelope and produced folded scraps that revealed his efforts '*avec la langue de Shakespeare*': they were like slightly weird folk songs. He once took a fortnight's trip to India, telling his sister he was visiting a friend in Picardy and phoning her every so often. 'She'd ask me how the weather was up north and I'd say, sweating like a pig, "Still cold and rainy."'

It was Elie who explained to me a few years ago why two of the commune's principal families won't talk to each other. At war's end, the local Resistance group had to deal with an eighteen-year-old collaborator from the village. They drew straws to find the executioner. The youngster who drew the shortest straw was also from our village. He took his schoolmate off into the scrub and shot him. 'Which families?' I asked, faux-naively. Elie smiled: 'To ask that question, you have to be either a Parisian or an Englishman.'

'I'm both,' I laughed.

The Germans laid their main telephone cable to Spain through the village, its anaconda-like remains still visible on the rougher tracks; it was revealed running some 50 yards below our house when some works were done on the lane. It ran right in front of Elie's farm, too, and when the men from the Resistance came one night, Elie's mother pleaded for it to be sabotaged further away. They conceded. He brushes at some dead leaves with his boot and a small numbered plaque appears. 'Look – those Germans were so efficient,' he says. 'The Alsaciens were friendly enough, though. One officer sat me on his knee in our kitchen and said I reminded him of his little blonde boy back home.' I wondered at what point simple expediency – his mother's pleading, the friendly officer in the kitchen – might become interpreted as a collaborative tendency. Certainly, Elie despises the village and the village does not think much of him, but this might be for quite other reasons.

A village is a complex tangle of heaped twigs and branches, I reflected recently, as I began making inroads with handsaw, telescopic loppers and secateurs into the small stuff that the village woodsman had left me to deal with after tidying up our trees. It was all destined for the hearth – actually, a large wood-burning stove. Twigs for kindling, thicker branches for the fire proper, to be added to the sawn lengths of log waiting in the cellar and stacked outside against the back wall for winter. Villages resist such ordering, thankfully, outside tyranny or war.

Speaking of which, Elie never attends our Armistice Day ceremony, which takes the form of a tour in the school minibus driven by the mayor. In 2012, an act of parliament instructed that 11 November should honour *'tous les Morts pour la France'* and not just those of the Great War. Our village has long done so, the mini-pilgrimage pausing at the two places where locals were killed by the occupiers in 1944, before it reaches the main *hommage* in the cemetery, with a coda of cloudy pastis in the *mairie*. It feels like a polite cloth drawn over the unhealed wounds and seething enmities, with only the minute's silence resonant with unsaid things.

When I first took part some 20 years ago, there were several veterans of 1939–45 still present, just as my father eventually became the last representative in his adopted village in Berkshire. Maurice told me that he had literally no stomach following his storming of a machine-gun nest in 1940. Sitting on the edge of the village fountain – its brass tap emerging from the wall of the *mairie* – he lifted his shirt to show the puckered scar, like a half-buried rope, running from flank to flank.

'How do you eat then, Maurice?'

'The surgeons left me just enough to keep drinking,' he joked. He spent most days in the café, downing pastis.

It was Maurice who told me that you could slip from one end of the village to the other via its cellars, intercommunicating by secret passages from the Camisard era. Our own back cellar has a recess covered in chicken wire, ostensibly for rabbits, separated from the neighbour's house by the thinnest of walls. One kick and you'd be through, dragoon or SS soldier left empty-handed.

Alain, with a poodle as white as his shock of hair, had witnessed the '*coups de feu*' in front of the eight-sided Protestant *temple*. Quite by chance, three *maquisards* (members of the French Resistance operating from the *maquis* or 'bush') had arrived from their mountain hideout in a clattery Citroën just as a German convoy of troop carriers and armoured cars was emerging from the narrow main street. Instead of pulling in, the Citroën reversed in a panic and was summarily dealt with by the lead machine-gunner. The car finished in the ditch and its occupants on the big table in the *mairie*, their guts (according to our neighbour) dangling down and touching the floor. The schoolchildren were forced to file past and look. The car was torched where it lay and the convoy moved on. Teenage Alain then joined the Maquis.

Not every account of those days is so memorable: when we first arrived and for the next decade or so, veteran Resistance members were almost two-a-penny. They were tough, and would be around forever with their tales, it seemed. Recently, when there was almost none left, I interviewed (for a BBC radio documentary) a local Resistance leader in his late eighties, who had seen a lot of action. He was perfectly compos mentis, but everything he said was dull. Ambushing the Waffen-SS, in his minimal account, was as thrilling as a trip to the supermarket.

The deadly spot is now marked by a small stone, its inscription blunt with anger: '*Ici ont été tués par les Allemands . . .*' This rather blunt statement ('Here the Germans killed . . .') is always the first shrine, although these days it's been shoved a few feet to the right by a modern villa's metal fencing. A medal-heavy veteran (not old enough for the Second World War) holds the banner, a large bouquet is laid, and the same bugle player for the past 20 years – a plump woman with short hair and sideburns whom I long mistook for a teenage boy – struggles through the Last Post.

Next stop: the stone bridge over the stream. In 1944, middle-aged Marcel was on his way to the café to pick up eggs for his mother, when the jittery occupants of an armoured car, approaching from behind, screamed a few *Verbotens*, the common signal to jump into the ditch with your hands up. Marcel, stone deaf from birth, ambled on. His body, riddled by bullets, was casually hurled over the bridge. We gather below the memorial stone, set high up on the bank and rarely without flowers.

The mayor always gives the little speech by the monument up in the cemetery. Last time, despite parliamentary instruction, he stressed the First World War, backed up by the unfaded porcelain photographs of its many local victims, kept under glass in a large iron-framed showcase beside the column. As usual, however, we remembered the village mother killed in Nîmes hospital when the city was bombed by the Americans. The olive trees rustled in the silence.

The wreath had been placed by two little girls roughly its size; I remember the time my equally diminutive daughter (now in her twenties) was assigned this task along with her best friend. On that occasion, the minute's silence was broken by old Gilbert: waving his arms, he shouted that he could still hear the bells pealing out on the same day in 1918. 'Everyone was rushing into the streets yelling about peace and victory – and my mother was in floods of tears. I couldn't understand it!' It was an extraordinary outburst, a cold rush of historical air as well as a sort of gift to the gathering. Gilbert did not survive that winter.

Last year's ceremony had its own bonus: Monsieur Jouve, a retired builder with a touch of the Protestant *illuminé*, took me through the many names on the monument after I had noted that one of them shared his own. 'This Jouve was a very distant cousin,' he said. 'My father, however, went right through the war – Verdun, the Dardanelles, you name it – and survived with just a graze on his forehead. On the front line, hand-to-hand combat, the lot. But he died prematurely of hepatitis, his liver like an alcoholic's. So the war did get him in the end. You know what his worst experience was? Coming back here on leave for nine days. It was the thought of returning to that hell. When the hell was all he had, it was bearable.'

That reminds me of boarding school, I commented. We agreed that the steep green valleys of the Cévennes do feel paradisal in the right light. Back in the *mairie*, we gathered around the big old table and sipped our pastis. Monsieur Jouve cornered me and talked serious life-philosophy for half an hour, tinted by religion. I nodded politely, helplessly conjuring what the table had once displayed some seven decades before, the dark liquids pooling on the very same bare-boarded floor.

5

Our Baker Is Missing

When our *boulanger* vanished some years back, the villagers hung about as Parisians might do in a catastrophic power cut: the bakery stood dark and forlorn, with no explanatory note on the door. Alain had got up at 2.30 a.m., six days a week, year in year out, and since he had teamed up with Lisa, had been utterly reliable in the way bakers should be. Pre-Lisa, Alain was unshaven, his baguettes singed, his croissants unavailable because he had slumbered until five. But with the firm hand of the *pâtissière*, whose cakes were divine – rich and creamy without being filling – Alain had got his act completely together.

The village admitted that this was because Lisa was from the north: they do things differently up there. For a start, Northerners know how to work. We Southerners, goes the refrain, regard work as something inconvenient between siestas, meals and pastis. On arriving some years before, Lisa had married the village restaurateur, Yves, nephew to the then mayor. Yves's copious menu had not changed for ages, and neither had the prices, so the restaurant was always full (as it still is). Lisa, possibly frustrated by this, promptly left him for the baker next door. There her considerable energy transformed Alain's domain from a gloomy room sporting the customary few loaves to a vibrant establishment selling honey, eggs, quiches, local books and crafts, and the aforementioned cakes.

Most striking of all to a casual visitor, though, are the paintings. Lisa paints in oils and acrylics every day. She built a studio in the barn at the back and adores the smell of turps and paint. 'Even white spirit does something to me,' she once told me. Her paintings, some of them very large, go through phases and differing influences (currently Edward Hopper) but, whatever the subject, are always bold and brilliantly coloured. You order bread with a huge, framed Alain staring at you as he cuddles a large cockerel. If you ask Lisa why, she gives you one of her cheeky smiles, the twinkle in her eye positively dazzling, and says, 'It just came to me.'

For a year or so she went through a 'dream' phase, and the imaginary landscapes were replaced by a seethe of naked bodies: Hieronymus Bosch crossed with the *Kama Sutra*. Some showed nudes engulfed in red flames or purple waves; others showed them blissfully interlacing in Douanier Rousseau-like undergrowth. She is prolific, the canvases stacked several deep or crowding every inch of wall, so I never quite know what might be facing me as I queue for croissants with the village's stumpy, stern old dears trailing their Calvinist heritage.

'Yes,' she reassured me one morning as I ordered her signature chestnut bread, 'I have strong dreams, but I don't interpret them.' Again the twinkle pulsed. 'I just paint them.'

Soon the dreams faded into Turneresque washes of golden light in which a few surreal figures floated, reminding me of near-death experiences as reported by survivors, and I wondered if the inspiration had gone. Fortunately, she began to take classes and veered into *plein-air* landscapes. (I bought one.) She obsessively depicted not only our hills, fields and lanes but neighbouring villages and their markets in the same vibrant hues that had little to do with the region's sombre Protestant colour scheme; going in for a loaf or a dozen eggs past the jolly cut-out figure of a baker was to put on a pair of new lenses.

But even Lisa has to have a break, and every year she goes up north, leaving Alain in sole charge. Since this involves serving as well as baking when no one else is available, things get a little erratic as the fortnight goes on. The difference that dramatic morning when the *boulangerie* remained shut was that a sleepy Alain did not appear at all. In fact, his white van was missing. Lisa was telephoned and had no idea where he might be, and neither did his extended family. Past sorrows in the latter meant that the police were alerted.

Soon the sound of helicopters disturbed the rural calm. Things were much more serious than an absence of bread. I watched the helicopters from our *terrasse*, with its view south almost to the sea. They were searching low, following the steep valleys, their blades fanning the limestone flanks of the hills and their sombre holm oaks. By the third day, we were fearing the worst. I imagined the *boulangerie* walls over the next few years covered in the equivalent of Goya's *Pinturas negras*. Lisa returned and was glimpsed looking anxious, but not despairing. She was an incorrigible optimist and was apparently cross with Alain for just hiving off without warning anyone. 'She can't face the reality of it,' was the general consensus.

On the fourth day, a phone call came and the news spread swiftly along the lanes. Alain's van had been spotted in Nîmes, where it was, coincidentally, the fourth day of the bullfighting *feria* – one of the biggest public festivals in Europe, when tens of thousands descend on the city and convert its streets into an extravaganza of drunken celebration while bulls die by the score in the vast Roman arena. Alain was found not far from his van, the back of which contained a sleeping bag and pillow: he was slouched at one of the many temporary *bodegas*, merrily consuming his umpteenth pastis, far from the blistering heat of the ovens, the trays, the dough in serried ranks, the night-time labour that made the profession one of the least popular to be apprenticed to back in the Middle Ages.

'Why shouldn't I enjoy myself?' was his first remark on being approached. 'Everyone else does.'

The key to it, we were told, was just walking out on everything and everyone. Planning and announcing a break would, he explained, have made everyone just as grumpy. How could he then enjoy it? Anyway, Lisa would never have let him. This way, the village was worried, not grumpy. They actually welcomed him back. They appreciated him. They noticed what a dreadful job it was, being a baker, and they couldn't blame him. Before, no one had seen past Lisa and her twinkle and her paintings to the gloomy engine-house where the real work happened. His going AWOL had been spontaneous. He'd taken nothing with him except the sleeping bag: no pyjamas, not even a toothbrush. Like a true wandering renegade, he stank on his return.

There were jokes about what Lisa's rolling pin would do to him once they were alone. She must have given him a big hug, and the huge 'Alain with cockerel' appeared soon after. Ever since, its subject has been much more cheerful, and we all make an effort to catch his eye and say, '*Bonjour, Alain, ça va?*'

When Lisa took a trip to London shortly afterwards, it was sensibly over a single weekend. I asked her what she was going to visit. 'Oh, only one place: the Tate Gallery.' (This was in the days before Tate Modern.) 'Good idea,' I enthused, waving my baguette. 'You'll love the Turner wing.' She frowned as she gave me my change. 'I'm only going to one room. Room 15. That's all I'm going all that way for. I've dreamed of it for years.' Room 15? 'The Surrealists, of course.' She sighed at my ignorance.

Between our village bakery and that single room hung with the likes of Dalí and Picabia and Paul Nash, there was a straight, unwavering line. Starting, as I fancied it, from Alain's weary eyes staring at me over the coxcomb.

6

Reprisal in the Oxbow

During our first three years in France, we lived in a small stone building which had once been an olive mill. It dated from the twelfth century, lay about half an hour nearer Nîmes than our present house, and we rented it for 2,000 francs a month. It stood on a near-island formed by an oxbow, or horseshoe-shaped *méandre*, the Vidourle river meandering dramatically between hills along that stretch. The term 'oxbow' dates from the fourteenth century, when it still meant an ox's collar, likening its curve in turn to a longbow; the subsequent riverine use was originally American and only dates from 1797, when I fancy that some imaginative pioneer looked at a map and had a synthesising moment. No prizes for visual accuracy, however. Our oxbow looked much more like the outline of a limp penis from the air than either a horseshoe or an ox's collar. Some locals called it a *larme*: a teardrop.

We spotted herons and buzzards above its heathy hectares, while everything from wild boar to grass snake busied itself among the clumps of holm oak, pine, alder and ash or scuffled between the modest rows of vines; in the river itself, otters, beavers and water rats joined the perch and trout and a legendary pike. Frogs and toads sang through the night, dippers flitted past our heads as we bathed. This scene of bucolic calm was misleading: the Vidourle is one of the most dangerous rivers in France, notorious for catastrophic floods, even after three flood retention dams were built. Occasionally, after heavy rain higher in the hills, the river would take a short cut and leave a drastic smear of thick sludge across the lower part of the U, cracking trees like twigs and uprooting mature specimens so that a path would be completely blocked.

I had never seen such devastation in my life before. Yet it soon settled back, the suspended clumps of dragged vegetation hanging like nests many feet over our heads, marking the maximum flood-level for several seasons. Down grassy, overgrown paths pungent with wild fennel, there were three or four spots suitable for swimming: we still use them from time to time. We reckoned it was an earthly paradise, even when failing to keep warm through the winters. Apart from an open fire and walls two feet thick, the mill was unheated. We were too broke to buy logs and brought back the remnants of broken trees – 'floodwater wood', as the drifter George calls it in Steinbeck's *Of Mice and Men*. This wood had to be sawn, and I only had a handsaw. The greed of the flames vied with the then-youthful energy of my forearm muscle, and almost won. The wood was sometimes suspiciously light – it had been rotting for years in riverside places where no one ventured – and was fairly useless as tinder. When I recently asked my grown-up children for their happiest memories of childhood, they immediately chose these firewood quests, and especially the return journey along the tracks in our clapped-out Renault estate, their small forms crouched in the front passenger footwell under trunks and branches draped in moss and waterweed.

I would walk every morning alone for an hour or more, finding a temporary space away from small children and domesticity and to reflect, teasing out the tangled threads of my writing (I had received a small advance for my first novel, and had a regular reviewing spot for the *Observer*). We bought a little fibreglass rowing boat second-hand, and childhood readings of *The Wind in the Willows* floated through my mind as I rowed up and down the long reach just a field's slope away from the house, working the oars right up to where the weir hissed: Ratty plopped out of sight yards from the hull, and there was the odd blue flash of kingfisher. This has to be better than the choking air of London, I reflected, whenever a certain sense of alienation, even isolation, crept in. Or, in other words, a fog on which the words *What on earth have I done?* were projected. I had left my full-time salaried teaching post and extended the sabbatical into something theoretically permanent. We had very few resources. We had moved country, leaving England so that I could continue with a novel set in deepest England. The poet Peter Porter, when I told him I was off to the Cévennes, looked alarmed. 'Oh my God,' he said, 'you'll never come back. We went there last year and saw peasants with hay forks silhouetted on a ridge. It was like a shot from Bergman's *Seventh Seal*.'

I did feel like a stray, and had a telling visitant in the form of a hunting dog that, for about a fortnight, followed me whenever I went out for a walk or a run. Its rib-cage showed like a balsa-wood frame under tissue. Once, when I found myself stumbling through thickening thorns, hopelessly lost, it led me back onto the right path.

Gérard, the tenant farmer who lived in the oxbow's cluster of farm buildings, reckoned the poor creature had cancer. 'I can smell it. The dog's dying.' I trusted Gérard. Once, after a fierce night of frost, which he'd mournfully predicted a few days earlier, I saw him in the field behind our house, crumbling what had been fresh vine leaves between his fingers. 'Look at this,' he said. 'I knew it. Glorified tobacco. I'll roll it for my *clope*.'

Then the dog vanished and I felt guiltily relieved.

Our neighbours, Jean and Maurisette from Brittany, were the *gardiens* for the large house adjoining ours, whose wealthy, ultra-right and Catholic owner was seldom present. Now in his sixties, broad-shouldered Jean had been a lorry driver before his delivery business went bust, and had fought in the French wars in Indo-China. He limped about mending everything, ignoring the lacerations on his hands when patching up a hole in our wire fence, climbing ladders despite the gammy leg, always beaming and dispensing advice, and ever wishing he was by the northern sea. He refused to talk in detail about the war. 'All war is horrible. No one realises unless they've been in one. What men do to each other. If the Yanks had asked me about Vietnam,

I'd have told them not to bother. It rained *comme vache qui pisse*, and it was hot. *Mon dieu, les moustiques!*'

They arrived the same day as us, by chance. They became our substitute parents, I suppose. Several evenings a week we would talk mostly politics over fragrant, fiercely strong pastis. We learnt much of what we needed to know about our adopted country from Jean and Maurisette. I think of them now as the last of the old France into which I was born in 1956, and that I remember so well from summer road-trips through the 1960s.

Each afternoon, our kids would happily trot up the short path to the couple's kitchen where a cornucopia of Haribo sweets, lurid *sirop* and trash telly awaited them.

So much for our dreams of rural purity.

An old friend came from London and stayed in a neighbouring farmhouse, part of which was empty. We walked together through the brush, heading for the river. Everywhere you went, apart from due north towards the road, you headed for the river.

'How on earth do you know where to go?' he asked.

I stopped. We were surrounded by bristly thickets, patches of thistles – all the scratchy, redolent stuff of Mediterranean scrub. 'I'm following the path,' I pointed out.

He smiled. 'What path?'

True, the path was no more obvious than an animal track, faint between the vegetation, imitated by countless others branching off, but I could distinguish it through familiarity as if it was waymarked in bright Dayglo paint.

'There,' I said, pointing.

'I believe you,' he laughed. I felt I'd arrived.

Our outside table was the old olive press, a great round cake of stone. A mule or two would have turned it, as the river was too far away from the crouch of our small vaulted building, whereas the tall ivy-clad mill on the opposite arm of the oxbow would have used the swift and powerful waters of the race – 'the white coal of the torrents of the Cévennes', as Emmanuel Le Roy Ladurie puts it in *The Peasants of Languedoc*. This 'supplemented' the black coal of Alès (still the capital of our region, though all the mines have closed). Mills would have been everywhere.

At the beginning of the eighteenth century, ours was the home of the local *curé*. Perhaps it was still functioning as a mill, and he'd wake to the squeak and grind of the wheel crushing olives below his bedroom, and the snorts of the mules. The priest's church stood two minutes' walk from us along a brambled track and was now a ruin. Holm oak saplings burst out of the walls, and overhanging branches of their older relatives provided the roof. I had to high-step through carpets of briar to reach the altar – or the slab I assumed had once acted as its base. I visualised a group of peasants out of a Courbet painting, in wooden clogs and threadbare shawls and with huge hands, clustering to enter and receive my blessing, to pray for rain or sun or a miraculous cure.

I have no idea whether our country priest was the simple, good man of my imagination. He might have been vicious: or just stubborn and self-righteous, or a loose-living alcoholic. Or a swirl of self-doubt, timidity and ineffectiveness, like the lonely hero of the 1930s novel by Georges Bernanos, *Diary of a Country Priest*, from which Robert Bresson made his first major film in 1950: intense and luminous in its black-and-white gloom, it shows the idealistic young man disintegrating under the parish's burden of cruelty and indifference and his creeping cancer.

Our own man's end was more abrupt. The oxbow's hamlet, just like the village further into the hills where we eventually settled, was a victim of big history. The Cévennes, and Languedoc in general, had taken to Protestant reform from its earliest days in the 1520s. At the beginning of the 1700s, after much tit-for-tat violence and increasing oppression,[1] some ten thousand Protestant rebels, mostly Cévenol and of a mystical, millenarian bent, held off some two hundred thousand troops loyal to the absolutist Catholic king,

[1] Louis XIV was an absolute ruler whose personal religion was also the nation's. Under the influence of the Jesuits, he began to turn against the two million industrious Huguenots busy modernising the country's economy. Eventually, with the revocation of the Edict of Nantes in 1685, he made Protestantism illegal, forced Huguenots to renounce their faith and embarked on a programme of outright persecution. Neighbouring countries received the resulting flood of refugees (including my own maternal ancestors, the Pinders, who ended up in Ireland) with mixed feelings, although this soon changed when they saw the outcome.

Louis XIV. They achieved this by the usual method of the freedom fighter (or terrorist, depending on your point of view): using an intimate knowledge of the local terrain or what Robert Louis Stevenson called 'their intricate hills'. They ransacked, ravaged or killed, then vanished. The Guerre des Camisards (the insurgents were so called from their white shirts or *camisoles*) dragged on for years, prolonged partly by the fact that many of the royal army's officers were reluctant to confront fanatical peasants fired by the Holy Spirit, and risk dying ingloriously in some godforsaken mountain pass. It wouldn't have looked good on the tombstone. And there were the incidental pleasures of life under the southern sun.

You have to be careful who you say this to in our area, but it's a sad fact that massacres of men, women and children happened on either side, as did material destruction. It is a depressingly long and vindictive history, transported across the Atlantic when war-weary idealists from both sides sought Utopia in America and continued to be wiped out and to retaliate in kind. When the Huguenots famously revenged themselves on the Catholics of Nîmes back in 1567, the deep well in the courtyard of the episcopal palace was full to the brim with dead and dying dignitaries, their throats summarily slit. The cathedral had already been ransacked and despoiled of its 'idols' years before, and was to suffer again – notably in 1621, when, in the name of purification, the altars and fonts were defecated on and Christ's image slashed with pikes. The present edifice, amputated of one of its towers, is so battered and voided out that its main attraction is the vestige of an eleventh-century Genesis narrative on the façade, with Adam and Eve clutching huge fig leaves over their parts, alarmingly close to St Michael's giant sword. These opening scenes of the frieze are almost miraculous, and I gaze up at them often. Vandalism could be ecumenical: the original Gothic entrance was replaced by an absurd classical portico when deemed too low for the visit of the Duchess of Angoulême (daughter of the unfortunate Louis XVI), who naturally had to enter on a dais, sporting her characteristic plume of feathers.

Louis XIV did things thoroughly. If he had had the defoliant Agent Orange at his disposal, he would have used it just as readily as the Americans did in the Vietnam War; instead he agreed with Nicolas Lamoignon de Basville, the ruthless intendant of Languedoc, to empty over 30 parishes of their inhabitants up in the higher, remoter hills and reduce the zone to ashes.

'This land of persecution and reprisals,' as Robert Louis Stevenson called it in *Travels with a Donkey in the Cévennes*, thinking perhaps of the vicious aftermath of the Jacobin rebellion. The mountains certainly resemble the Highlands in places, with the most distant peaks fading into pale blue cut-outs, like a Chinese silkscreen, layer upon layer. What makes the Camisard rebellion distinctive, however, is its mystical Calvinism, with a hint of the apocalyptic. There was much falling onto knees, singing of psalms on marches, gabbling prophecy, inspired sermonising, breathless evidence of miracles, with the murmurings of secret mass assemblies worshipping in caves 'in the Desert', like the earliest Christians. Decisions were often made by angelic intervention, a silvery voice in the ear. As in later guerrilla warfare, women were fully involved, not only supplying the rebels with food and arms, but fighting alongside them. Prophetesses were particularly valued, and according to the contemporary reports (written, it has to be said, by men), often showed themselves more vengeful against captured individuals, obeying the furious whispers in their heads.

The most intense fighting occurred in a relatively small area of the mountains and foothills, spreading itself like a gunpowder trail towards Nîmes, passing beside the oxbow. The Camisard story still inspires a certain *fierté*, an anti-Parisian sentiment of proud localism, and has made not only romantic figures of leaders like Rolland, Cavalier or Bonbonnoux, however ruthless they were in practice, but symbols of freedom of expression, of liberty. It is also more safely distant in time than local tales of the Maquis. Stevenson found himself 'well looked upon' for being Protestant, as have I, however lapsed my faith. One farmer clapped me warmly round the shoulder and cried, 'We are the same family!' I have to add that we were considering buying a dilapidated house belonging to his late mother, the attics full of old farm tools. Not only could we not afford it, but (on local enquiry) one charred room stinking of soot turned out to be where she'd been murdered in her bed by a passing vagrant, who had attempted to burn her corpse. That night I dreamed the whole thing from her point of view with extraordinary vividness. I woke up with a cry and told Jo, 'I was having my afternoon nap, the shutters were closed, he came in wielding a huge kitchen knife.' These last three facts, unknown to us, turned out to be true. There is much in these hills that broods beyond the rational grasp, or momentarily passes on a soft whistle of ecstasy up on the peaks.

Reprisal certainly claimed our *curé de campagne*. Had he persecuted others, or was he simply on the wrong side, like Graham Greene's whisky priest? We stood on the spot with our Protestant landlady, who lived further up the lane in a solid, square chateau built in 1901 by her grandfather. 'Look carefully,' she said, pointing to the left of the back door, 'you can still see the bullet-holes.' I would repeatedly examine the wall's rough stone, infilled with dollops of lime plaster and mud, but the marks of lead balls from flintlock pistols or muskets fired over three centuries before seemed more the product of imagination. She insisted that she was shown them by her grandfather 50 years earlier.

I had much less difficulty picturing the priest being dragged from his supper by gaunt, unshaven men, then thrust against the outside wall, his legs shaking under the cassock. Three or four very loud explosions, acrid puffs of smoke, a slumped form on the ground. It was a minor, even typical incident of the conflict, when thousands perished on both sides. Louis XIV's dragoons took two years (from 1702 to 1704) to flush out the rebels led by the mythical Rolland, despite his belief that all they needed to guard them in the mountains was a few angels. They were extraordinarily skilled at vanishing into the bush. The only surprise was that our modest medieval building hadn't been torched, but they reserved that punishment for the church up the lane, and for the much larger parish church in the next village. Perhaps our mill was indeed torched and the thick-walled shell rebuilt, as (according to Henri Bosc, the leading historian of the wars) several mills, a farmhouse, stables and a barn, all standing within our isolated oxbow commune, were recorded as being burnt down on 9 March 1703.

It seemed that the rebels favoured the banks of our river for a period; given that the old Roman road to Nîmes runs roughly parallel to its course for a while, it was an obvious target for disruption and terror exploding out of the hills. One attack involved around thirteen hundred 'Children of God'. Perhaps we must imagine our priest confronted by a massed horde – a great yelling mob, from his point of view. Around the same time, the rebels not only burnt down a neighbouring farmstead but hanged its unfortunate farmer, having removed his testicles, tongue and eyes. Such acts were always done by God's command. One presumes the farmer was a Catholic informer, and not a hapless innocent. Or were his killers the notorious Catholic *milice*, disguised as Camisards and keen on sowing hatred via such outrages?

Outrages could be official. Captured rebels were broken on the wheel limb by limb, sometimes en masse, or lowered into a blazing pyre on a wooden hoist, suitably within sight of the Roman arena in Nîmes (a largely Protestant city). Loutish dragoons were lodged with villagers and not only abused their hosts but reported them if they failed to attend mass: the punishment was the galleys, where you were chained to your bench and oar for six months, day and night. 'Exterminating' selected villages was a frequent command from on high. The war followed us, as it were, when we moved after three years to our present home deeper in the hills; as mentioned previously, the lower part of the village had been thus dealt with in September 1703, as a punishment for receiving the rebels and '*pour servir d'exemple*'. Two thousand of them had apparently been spotted (one could probably divide this eyewitness exaggeration by at least two), yet before the mounted dragoons arrived, trotting up from their fort a few miles away, the whole lot had vanished.

Not that the rebels ever gave the villagers much choice, whatever their sympathies: two months before, the Camisards had entered the high street firing muskets and yelling 'Kill! Kill!', capturing up to 10 inhabitants 'and a mule'. All were released the next day, including the mule.[2]

Earlier in the year, Rolland had smashed up the church, then summarily killed the headmaster of a nearby school,

[2]No doubt as much a subsequent topic of conversation as poor Matt's mule in Zora Neale Hurston's masterpiece *Their Eyes Were Watching God*, whose description of life in an incorporated Black village in 1930s Florida feels so eerily familiar.

presumably for inculcating the old, unreformed faith in young Cévenol minds. Our higher part of the village was where the troops lodged, which explains why it survived intact. Their long slashing sabres were hopelessly unsuited to the narrow lanes and paths of the Cévennes, or against the flickering, agile natives. The large house adjoining our garden is still known as 'Le Fort', and our *quartier* was referred to disparagingly several times in our early years as the place from which they watched the rest burn. Some of the older residents maintained (having heard this from a grandparent, usually) that the houses – including our own – were commandeered by force, others that the families were quislings. Given our panoptic view to the south, and the presence of a secret, false-bottomed hiding place or *cachette* – suitable for a large Bible or a small person – in the venerable wall cupboard in what had once been the main room (now my study), a further legend that our house in particular was a Camisard meeting place seemed equally plausible. The *cachette* now holds my own family Bible, a great leather-bound pack of rag-paper pages from the early nineteenth century, the sole surviving souvenir from that generation.

Nothing of the lower village above the ground floor dates from earlier than 1703. Two and a half centuries later, the Waffen-SS were to sweep through the mountains in similar fashion, equally savage, equally frustrated, thundering up the old Roman road from Nîmes through the dawn cold. According to our landlady, our oxbow hamlet was used as a local headquarters by the Gestapo: this was confirmed by the

octogenarian onion-grower in the market, who recalled
the fact with a shudder.

Our first smoky winter in the mill was a struggle to keep
warm, until we bought a wood-burning stove. I had
almost finished *Ulverton*, writing in a room in the eaves.
One afternoon, there was a gentle knocking on the
glassed entrance, whose semi-circular form followed
the curve of the vaulting. A small, chubby man in a black
cassock was hovering. His dress reminded me a little of
the bats that occasionally swooped into the house, their
terrifying faces apparently aimed at ours, which were
dutifully terrified in turn. This man's face, however,
was mild. I tried not to think of Bresson's film.
   'I have come to see the martyr's house,' he said.
   I had no idea what he meant, at first. He explained.
So the story was true after all.
   Showing him the infamous spot by the back door,
I apologised for my failure to find the traces of lead
shot. 'This is an important house,' he said, rubbing his
spectacles on his sleeve. 'The site of his terrible end.
A place for pilgrimage. Those Protestant fanatics!
I'm the parish priest, by the way. I've been intending
to come here for years.' I had the impression that the
shooting had happened a few months back, or at least
within a lifetime, like the murders and massacres of
the last war. I told him somewhat apologetically that
I was an Anglican, at least in theory. He waved his
hand dismissively and we chatted over a bottle of wine.
The locals were not terribly interested in Christ, he

complained. He appeared resigned to disappointment. He was the only pilgrim we ever saw.

I didn't feel completely fraudulent in front of him: having small children encouraged us to lighten their existential burden with a spoonful of faith. Bible stories and the odd harmless prayer before bed laid down seams of cultural knowledge and metaphysical reassurance, if nothing else. No French (non-Catholic) state school ever touched such things, obeying the secular rules dreamed up after centuries of forced religious teaching: this seemed to me a dereliction of cultural duty.

One evening, after a year or so in France, my eldest son (aged four) asked, 'Where is God, exactly?' 'In everything.' 'Even in trees?' 'Yup.' 'So if He's in a tree, is He in the trunk, branches or the leaves?' 'Well, He's sort of in the trunk and branches and leaves at the same time. And He – I mean, She – might be female. An Earth Mother.' He pondered. 'Every single leaf?' 'Er, yes.'

He reflected a moment. 'OK, but then where would He be standing?'

I saw his point. 'Our minds are too small to know how it all works,' I faltered. Maybe Buddhism or paganism would have been easier. Life as a river with no beginning and no end, impossible to grasp. My son has been a confirmed sceptic through the two and a half decades since.

No doubt the ghost of the priest, said to linger by the back of the mill, might have helped me out.

7

The Psychological Castle

Guillaume is standing on the little concrete bridge over the stream, a billhook in his right hand and a pair of handcuffs dangling from his left wrist. He is like the troll in a folk story, guarding access to the world beyond – in this case, the continuation of a favourite walk around the village, winding through holm oaks, vineyards and a stone-built farm whose dog is tiresomely incapable of recognising me as anything but an extreme threat.

Our troll is, in fact, one of the village's few genuine *soixante-huitards*, leaving Paris for the Cévennes mountains at the age of 18 when the tear gas had barely cleared. In the summer of 1968, our valley was a favourite with the utopians thanks to a semi-derelict *manoir*, soon populated by every stripe of rebel. A few stayed on. When I first met Guillaume some 20 years back, he was a jobbing gardener. Our kindly then-neighbours, Georges and Michelle, had hired him for a few hours a week. Guillaume would arrive in his battered green van and mess about for an hour or two. He loved bonfires, clipping branches and creating thick, acrid smoke.

If you caught his eye through the pittosporum, he would buttonhole you with stories interspersed with epigrammatic wisecracks that recalled Cioran, the Romanian philosopher whose intense pessimism manages to be refreshing in the face-burning way of a Siberian wind. Guillaume didn't know Cioran, but would have agreed with him that 'Society is not a disease, it's a disaster', and that to believe and hope is 'to lie to oneself'.

Seeing the world as a ship of fools can make you a recluse; although Guillaume had a wife and daughter, he seemed to illustrate Cioran's observation that 'you cannot protect your solitude if you cannot make yourself odious'. A passion for women erupted in sudden lubricious remarks, semi-camouflaged in a chuckling Parisian argot.

He was also perky back then, proud that he had stayed on in the hills while 'most of the other kids went back up to their mums and dads the minute it got cold'. Beardless, with a mischievous smile and crooked beret, he didn't look like the other *babas*, as the French call anyone vaguely hippie-like (from a combination of the Hindi for 'papa' and the French for 'stupefied'). He did, however, imbibe, and often turned up with his outdoor flush deepened to carmine. His wife left him, and the house was sold. Before leaving it for the last time, he carefully painted a long Latin citation on the garage doors, which I meant to get round to asking him about. It felt like a curse. After a period of serious drinking and collateral oddity, he built a two-room bungalow on a plot of land he'd kept on the other side of the dirt track, overlooking the solar-panelled house now occupied by second-homers from Montpellier.

Both rusty billhook and plastic handcuffs are clues to Guillaume's obsession, or what he has called 'my illness': he can't stop collecting junk. His pickings and purchases have now overwhelmed the bungalow, sneaked along the approach path and started to accumulate in fusty heaps on his ribbon of land between an olive grove and a wooded slope. 'I know where everything is,' he once claimed, gazing into his now dismantled metal shed – bursting with his booty. He reassured me that he was not a miser, like the equally compulsive hoarder Plyushkin in Gogol's *Dead Souls*. 'It's my cocooning urge. Lack of mother-love.' Once, after proudly showing me a headlamp reflector found in a ditch, Guillaume suddenly said, 'I'm old, on my own, and broke. I never bothered about my pension. Capitalist, I thought. I'm 63, *merde*. I smashed up a car a year, until the judge told me to stop drinking or it's prison. I haven't touched a drop in ages. It's torture.'

'You're not old, Guillaume,' I ventured, the dystopian rain dripping off the branches. 'And you seem quite cheerful.'

'Antidepressants.' His eyes brightened suddenly. 'I'm reading Céline. Genius. And a book about Mouna. Aguigui Mouna? My entire philosophy of life. A one-man demo on a bicycle. Flowers in his beard. A mixture of Don Quixote, Diogenes and Jesus. Ecology? He was there first!'

The bungalow, concealed beyond an olive grove belonging to an old lady in the village, seems an emanation of Guillaume himself; you can see what is now a hefty serpent of junk as a long and sinuous phrase, beginning with a First World War stretcher and ending on the large exclamation mark of a roadworks warning sign clambered over by small teddy bears. I have seen worse in exhibitions of contemporary art. I am jealous of the stretcher: I have a leather-bound trench flask and field binoculars that belonged to my grandfather, who survived the first day of the Somme and several weeks of Passchendaele in the 2nd Hampshires before being invalided home, but a stretcher is something else.

Despite present appearances, Guillaume is not a threat. He says he is clearing the stream, and I note a few inroads made into the bank's thick growth of alder and buckthorn. 'I'm worried,' he says, waving his billhook close to my nose, 'I am almost become a *normaliste*, when I am really a *normalophobe*.' 'I don't think clearing a stream voluntarily is that normal, these days,' I say, 'but watching the telly might be.' He snorts. 'I don't have a telly, *mon cher*, I have books.'

His ensuing patchwork of argot and polemic contains the real reason why he is getting his boots wet: long ago when he was a little boy, he would walk to his Paris school as the gutters were being sluiced. All he wanted to do was to dam them up like the older boys and sail paper boats, but his mother would drag him away. 'We are always being dragged away from our desires,' he sighs, shaking his handcuffs. 'Now I am re-enacting it all.'

I tell him that my earliest memories of Paris are likewise of pavements and gutters, the sound of dry leaves on the cobbles, along with enormous chrome bumpers. 'You're so low down,' I laugh, 'it's about all you notice.' He nods vigorously. I add that I have an almost sexual obsession with the Citroën DS from the 1950s. He looks at me as if I am peculiar.

We more often cross paths at our local town's *vide-grenier*, the equivalent of a British car boot sale and generally indistinguishable from the regular flea market, or *puce*. A snooty visitor from Paris once remarked that the town – grimly shabby in an atmospheric 1930s way – had the worst-dressed people he had ever seen. 'I mean, really poor. *C'est incroyable.*' 'Well, there's a lot of unemployment here,' I said. When I took a friend from London around the stalls, she couldn't believe it: 'But this is not even *junk*,' she cried. 'It's actual *rubbish*.' For a moment I saw it all through different eyes; not as an intriguing cross section of the past hundred years of Languedoc life, nor as a way for impoverished locals to keep their budget down with *des bonnes occases*,[1] but as clutter – the kind of stuff that no one could possibly want in their homes. You have to beware your presumptions, however: in the same town's *puce* last year, an artist friend (an expert collector) spotted an unframed sepia shot of Notre Dame cathedral among mattresses, glass flagons and TV sets, and bought it for 10 euros. Having already spotted the signature of Gustav Le Gray, the greatest French photographer of the nineteenth century, he had it valued in Paris at 10,000 euros.

[1] From *occasions*, meaning 'bargains' or 'second-hand goods'.

Three weeks before our bridge encounter, I found Guillaume standing in front of the spread jumble of a good friend who has become, to the despair of her husband, an obsessive flea-market trader. A full-time school secretary, Delphine gets up every Saturday and Sunday morning at three o'clock to be sure of a decent spot in one or other of the Cévenol markets. 'We need the extra cash,' she said. When they come round to supper these days, she has to leave early; I suggested that she must have an *amour* among the traders. This ribald remark did not go down well, although not because it might have been true: beyond any question of the modest gains she makes, she is simply addicted. As Guillaume is addicted to purchasing.

I greeted Delphine and turned to examine Guillaume's latest foundling: a heavy iron contraption with a wooden handle and a pedal that he claimed was a wine bottle corker. It was broken, which was why he'd bought it. 'It has to be useless or I'm not interested. I've worked through my savings, my pension, and now I'm eating into my life insurance.' His unlicensed, clapped-out Renault 5 was full of more stuff, including the complete set of a mossy nineteenth-century encyclopaedia that I felt vaguely envious of, until he told me what he'd paid for it. 'I offer *more* than they're asking,' he giggled, his crumpled hat falling over his eyes. 'I love to see their shocked faces. It troubles them. They think they're being cheated!'

Glued above the car's rear bumper was a large handwritten *REGISTER*. This was what poor Marie Durand, the teenage Protestant imprisoned by the

Catholics in the Tour de Constance in Aigues-Mortes from 1730 to 1768, carved into the cell's stone floor. It is thought to mean 'resister' in her local patois, but Guillaume has another theory. 'She made a mistake,' he said, pushing his latest purchase into the boot, 'even though she had plenty of time to correct it!' The original version still holds: a lycée student told me recently that his mother was on the bus some years ago wearing her Huguenot cross, when a man opposite raised his fist and cried, '*Register!*'

Back home, I checked to see how much an unbroken antique French wine bottle corker might set one back: £480. Irrelevant to Guillaume, because he never sells.

I sometimes wonder whether I, too, have a touch of Plyushkin syndrome. During our early years here in the Cévennes I would scavenge in the illegal dump sprawled in trees outside the village, not out of grim necessity like a Third World waste picker but for discarded items of the old country ways. Clambering over the festering huddles of fridges, tyres, mangled chairs, mattresses and (for some reason) numerous toilet bowls, I eventually found, under warped sheets of plasterboard, a shallow reed-woven basket with a string for a handle, once used for gathering mushrooms or chestnuts. I was delighted. Stationed on our balcony, it started to swell and loosen. When Guillaume came round one day and saw it, his eyes lit up, but it disintegrated in his hands. '*Alors ça, c'est comme la vie,*' he said. This felt like a found poem, and I promptly wrote it out when he had left. In some sense, poets are hoarders anyway, foraging through memory or life itself for multimodal scraps: a number of my poems feature such pickings as their literal subject. It was Guillaume who identified an ugly folding spade that I'd unearthed in one of our cellars as military, a US army entrenching tool from the last war. His nose flared as though at something delicious through his hunger. I still find it ugly, but won't part with it.

There is a difference between 'collecter' and 'collectionner' lost in the usual translation: 'to collect'. Guillaume's thousands of objects are not a collection, or his sensitivity to their textures, the aesthetic and philosophical connections he makes between them, would bring him close to being an *art brut* artist: the enviable stretcher from the First World War, propped outside his door, is on the same level as a broken toy tractor. I once suggested, in teacher mode, that this could all edge towards artistic status, if he were to add a pinch of intention. 'That would destroy the whole point,' he scoffed. 'It gives it all a meaning!'

Today, on the bridge, he is mourning the death of François Cavanna at 90. Writer, cartoonist, ecologist, founding editor of *Charlie Hebdo*'s predecessor, the satirically cruel and outrageously scatological magazine *Hara-Kiri* (Cavanna reckoning hara-kiri 'the height of stupidity'), Guillaume's working-class hero had the kind of tumultuous and tormented Parisian life which Guillaume deliberately escaped by fleeing to the Cévennes hills as a youth in 1968. When I profess ignorance of Cavanna, he splutters in disbelief. 'But you're a writer too! Yes, yes, I understand, *d'accord*, you're much too busy scribbling your little books that almost no one opens anyway . . .'

The average bookshop holds 50,000 titles, and I'm relieved if one of them is mine, but I say nothing. Now and again Guillaume's babbling words, like the proverbial troll's, cut sharply.

A few months later, *Charlie Hebdo* was to become internationally known as the bloody target of Muslim fundamentalists, since when a succession of similar horrors has pitched us all into a different world, although not one unfamiliar to historians of religion.

As if following suit, the olive grove that glinted and glowed its silvery green and which provided Guillaume and his bungalow with a covert, has mostly gone. D. H. Lawrence recognised the difficulty of capturing, in words or paint, 'the lovely glimmer of olive trees'. Van Gogh managed it, despite declaring, 'It's too beautiful for me to dare to paint it.' He found that 'the murmur of an olive grove has something very intimate, immensely old about it'. The old lady who owned the acreage thought similarly, and would come up especially to walk between the gnarled boles. She died last year, in her nineties. She had held out against her children's demands to sell the patch. Within weeks, it seemed, they had parcelled it up in as tight a mosaic of *terrains constructibles* as they could legally manage, in an area with a severe shortage of new housing. I had envisaged two villas at most, but there are now five.

Perhaps in response, Guillaume's serpent of junk has writhed and fattened, spreading into a kind of rampart. ('It's my psychological castle,' he once explained.) Now it is spilling over the stone walls in a riot of barely distinguishable items, from broken cane chairs to old prams and tin buckets, topped by a cathode-ray TV ('I never watch telly'). There is only just enough space for his rattling Renault, one wing-mirror tightly bound in red, white and yellow tape.

At first I imagined that the huge backhoe digger parked on the public track was his *pièce de résistance*, as it was festooned in teddy bears, rubber ducks and red ribbons, with a handwritten cardboard sign at its foot declaring MARCHE EN AVANT – perhaps a wry glance at soon-to-be-President Macron's *En Marche* movement. Eventually I realised that this ungainly machine was there only for the new houses, and Guillaume was making a temporary feature eccentric and therefore palatable.

It has now gone, the last villa all but finished. Perhaps the digger did, after all, 'walk forward' on its caterpillar tracks. The *mairie* has promised the proud new house-owners that the unsightliness will be dealt with, but nothing has changed. Meanwhile, I am struck by a surprising addition to the swelling junk outside: a tall and pretty house-plant in its pot. Fresh and green in this hot summer, it must be getting regularly and even lovingly watered.

8

Taking the Postman Hostage

While their British counterparts are studying comparative religion from primary school onwards, French children learn about the political system, finishing with a year of philosophy. This perhaps explains a certain official tolerance of intelligent protest, with a historic fondness for the barricade. I was amazed some years ago to see an alpine ridge of chairs heaped up in front of a Nîmes lycée for a fortnight. Montpellier University was similarly blocked for an entire semester in response to what appeared to be a minor change in researchers' conditions. While infuriating if you're trying to follow a cursus – especially as militancy tends to attract the least assiduous – *le blocage* remains a sign of democratic health, a historic right extending to the remotest village in the mountains.

Take ours, for instance. When that chronic threat to shrink the school by a whole class was about to be enacted, the teachers, parents and pupils protested with sit-ins, huge home-made banners draped across the façade and railings, and a journey to Nîmes to confront the *préfet*. We were told to 'bring things that make a noise', which meant a timeless recourse to pots and pans. The class was retained, the school predictably expanding with its reputation for being *dynamique*, and now an environmentally friendly school has been built at huge cost (much of it EU-funded) in the field below, sporting a vegetal roof like a hanging garden, and with inner walls of healthy pale-brown clay on which it is impossible to pin anything up.

More drastic methods are sometimes used, which in Britain would probably risk a jail sentence. Fracking has been dropped by the government as a result of protests, and a beautiful local valley (where we often swim) was saved from being dammed and flooded when the first two earth-movers were set on fire. Holding the manager of a doomed factory in his office for days is one favourite.

A variant was shown in our village some years ago, in relation to its then-full-time post office. Tucked below the church, in a building housing a cellar that was once the local lock-up (a service no one fought to retain), its dwindling use led to rumours of imminent closure. Our hard-left mayor at the time called on the villagers to gather in front of La Poste half an hour before the postman was due to arrive to collect the mail. We did, with appropriate banners, although the political effectiveness of impressing a postman seemed doubtful.

The yellow Renault van turned up on the sloping lane in the usual squeal of tyres, and the *facteur* – a jolly, portly character – passed through our chanting ranks with a diplomatic wave. He disappeared through the front door into the tiny bureau behind the counter, where the elderly post office lady awaited him with the mailbags.

The mayor and his accomplices then sprang into action, surging into the building and telling us to follow. The size of the room meant that it was full within seconds, like a crowded Métro carriage. The postman, trapped in the bureau behind with the embarrassed clerk, was told to phone HQ and inform them that he had been kidnapped by the village *citoyens* in protest at the planned closure, and would not be released until management had agreed to meet said citizens for a proper discussion.

Whenever I am caught up in such moments, part of me stands back and observes the swirl of action, taking mental notes for some future novel. Authenticity is important to me, and the unfolding excitements are hard to get right; saturated by fictional versions in film or TV dramas, one gropes for the real thing. Here, I would have expected the postman to be annoyed, even vaguely frightened. The hurtling speed of most postal vans is indicative not so much of impatience as of a desire to keep to designated collection times; an interruption like this produces a domino effect that might tumble the entire day. Instead, he was chuckling as he picked up the office phone (there was no mobile signal in the valley back then).

He told his superiors that he was blocked in our village through the action of the locals. I could tell from the long gaps that his superiors were both flummoxed and exasperated. I wondered if, when the police arrived, they would haul away everyone or just the leaders. I saw my head being pushed down into a squad car. What kind of jail sentence might the charge of hostage-taking attract? Surely, I thought, as the postman began to lose his chuckle on the phone ('I can't do anything about it! How can I just walk out? I'm trapped! I know it means everything gets held up, I'm not stupid! *Putain!*'), kidnapping a public servant in the course of his duties – especially the quasi-sacred mail collection – must be doubly serious. But any notion of sneaking away was happily scuppered: I was in the midst of the throng within, pressed against a poster announcing a range of bird stamps.

The postman, now looking anxious, handed over the phone to the mayor. A notoriously grumpy character with a farmer's arthritis and a rebel's Zapata moustache, Rémy surprised me by being friendly rather than defiant. He asked to speak to the boss of the whole region, and appeared to be joking with the lesser functionary on the other end. This did not please the *facteur*, who clearly felt left out and was rapidly declining into bourgeois individualism. The mayor came off the phone and told him that he would have to stay until the boss had called and given his promise. How long might that be? He had no idea.

'Then lock me in,' the postman said. 'Otherwise I'll get it in the neck for not trying hard enough.' So, at his request, he was locked up in the inner sanctum. To make things even easier for him, the van's tyres were deflated and the lane piled with the feature that had so far been missing: a barricade of breeze blocks and old school benches.

Most of us left the building and hovered in the lane or sat on the churchyard grass that overlooked the post office entrance. I recalled an old lady telling me how, in the old days (she remembered them vividly), this patch was a favourite resort for locals to relieve themselves in before the age of home toilets and septic tanks. Now only heedless dogs favoured it, but I was careful to check before I made myself comfortable. Over the next three hours, food and wine were passed to the hapless captive. This being France, he made appreciative remarks about the home-made victuals, and an intense conversation about the wine's qualities ensued. Then the door was locked again. Not a single *gendarme* had appeared, let alone the CRS – France's bulky riot police. We picnicked together, the birds hopped about. It was most convivial.

Finally, the phone rang. It was the big boss, of a *cadre supérieur*. The hierarchical nature of France was on full display: the promise was grudgingly extracted, the tyres were pumped up again, the barricade dismantled and the postman emerged into the sun. We all cheered him, clapping as he passed us. He beamed. This, I thought, would be a memorable moment in his life, something to recount in the bistro. We all like to be cheered, after all. His collection times were shot, the mail would arrive a day late, he'd be remonstrated with by each post office clerk in turn, but all he would have to say was, 'Kidnapped'.

The post office was allowed to stay open on the basis that an official *fréquentation* be kept, which led to frequent purchases of a single stamp. We opened an account there. Opening times contracted, protests rumbled on. Finally, a new medical centre meant the tatty old doctor's surgery could be converted into a shiny new Agence Postale Communale: open every morning till midday, it additionally provides a couple of computers, a printer and a fax machine. It sells goats-milk soap and books by local authors. Mine haven't exactly flown off the shelf, but the few that have gone are worth a hundred sales elsewhere.

9

Resident Tombs

A homestead's fortunes can be read in the outside walls: large wodges of dressed stone for good times, rubblestone for bad. Guy, our builder, was examining a side wall for the source of an ominous bulge and cracks. He pointed out the chest-high kernel in the left corner that the rest grew from, nestling against an outcrop of bare rock: 'Maybe a pig-house,' he said. 'Or for goats.' It consisted of just four or five roughly dressed but massive blocks. Successive waves and expansions were clear, like ripples, outlined in tell-tale gaps I could put my finger into. Amazed, I asked how old the pig-house was. '*Ouf*,' he chuckled, 'we could be talking *gallique*. Before the Romans! Very old, anyway.' His own fascination with history, ancient and recent, was coming into play. He was from Alsace, he told me; his Cévenol in-laws a generation back had added three Jewish children to their own nine, and no one had noticed.

We were originally a humble steading with outbuildings immediately in front and a field – a vineyard, in living memory – sloping down to the lane. The place was owned by Paul's childless uncle and aunt. Paul was still mayor when we first came and died in his eighties only a few years ago. His wife, Lydie, ran the café, like her mother and grandmother before her. Paul told me that the house was sold off in three portions – the house, the outbuildings in front, the land – and he disapproved of this avuncular profiteering. He reckoned our house was now a mere amputated limb of the original body, which had once been *beau*. 'That's why you got it for a song,' he said, with disarming frankness, as he couldn't understand why we'd bought it in the first place. He'd stand in my study and remember its heavy darkwood furniture, and the curtains that hid his aunt's bedroom towards the back, beyond an arch. 'My uncle slept where you've got your bathroom, next door.' That made sense: no natural light, and set so deep into the hill it keeps an even temperature: rocks bulge from the back wall. 'Almost a troglodyte,' he laughed. 'At any rate, they didn't sleep together. Not surprising there were no *gosses*.'

Paul had a point about the dividing up. A stone footbridge arching over the gennel, first included in the nineteenth-century land register as a mark not much bigger than a dash, connected the main house to the barn in front. The barn was now our neighbour's, the bridge technically no one's, but we had the *jouissance*. When it came to us deciding whether or not to buy, it was the view, the number of rooms and this Venetian touch that won us over. Three years later, the Venetian touch collapsed into rubble after a great clap of thunder during a storm, its many pumice stones already spongy from the infiltration of rain. At least, as Madame Mourier pointed out, no one was underneath. Despite not belonging to anyone, the remains were demolished at our expense and the rumour went round the village that the *Anglais* were architectural vandals. Without its buttress (or, depending on one's point of view, its more fatal drag), the building is placidly, minutely falling forward, and we follow the cracks with interest.

At the back, facing the cobbled gennel, our house consists of two separate but physically joined dwellings plus attached barn, which is definitely ours: the poverty of whoever owned the left-hand part can be seen in an added level of rubblestone and much thinner walls, as clear as César-Denis Daly's nineteenth-century parapet on Albi cathedral. That's why our bedroom – originally, when we arrived, a granary or storage loft with an earth floor – gets too cold in the winter and too hot in the summer. But it has the best view, reached by a further curve of uneven steps whose lime mortar I periodically have to mend. You can see the bottom of this staircase (too grand a term) from the cellar below, seemingly hanging in space. When I expressed my concern to Guy, he shoved in a prop: a plank of wood. I try not to think about it too much when going up to our bedroom. At the back of the barn, still full of stacked timbers from when we restored the collapsing roof, is a room I have only entered once, as it's difficult of access and contains the horrific-looking skeleton of a cat.

In the former goat-house at the front, where the previous owners had found a Roman tile, stands a great trough carved out of a single block of limestone, like a round church font, embedded in the rubblestone wall. It seems to be keeping the whole place up. It was full of goat dung when we arrived. Perhaps it dates from a long-ago period when the farmstead's affairs were more prosperous. Guy suggested that it was already there, a great isolated boulder in the middle of a field, and was simply carved out in situ. Then the house grew round it. 'Before the Romans, maybe. Who knows?'

Perhaps it *was* a font: recuperated features tend to turn up in the garden, too – corners of thick stone window-frames, for instance, that appear medieval. I once pulled out an iron bar in the shape of an extended U, and it served as a primitive pergola. Years later, Paul visited our garden to show me where the two old sisters who once lived in the back portion of our house were buried (being Protestant, they could be interred on their own land). He remembered them sitting on the door-sill and eating their gruel as he ran down to school. 'They'd always give me a wave. Poor as dirt, they were. The tomb was just there, with a railing around it. Now there's nothing.' I pointed at my pergola. 'Er, is that the railing?' He was quite shocked, until I explained. He said that the railing was perfectly intact when he'd last come up our garden steps to look, the tomb swept clean. 'When was that, Paul?' He frowned. 'Just after the war, I suppose,' he admitted.

They were lying several metres down, he reassured me, at the legal depth for a corpse. Following their death, a family of refugees from the Spanish Civil War moved in. Their bedroom became my daughter's over half a century later, with the same ancient beams and marks of nails where the curtain had been hung around the bed to give some privacy.

Before organised refuse collection came in some 40 or 50 years ago, waste – including the human sort – was deposited in your own plot. It took years before a corner of our garden was cleared of tangled metal, rusted cans, broken bottles, ancient pottery sherds and hundreds of little glass tubes like the debris of a heroin addict. Goat medication, someone said. The soil was of a dark, friable sort that may have been the result of decades, perhaps centuries, of human composting, including the Mourier family's waste. It can't have looked very pretty, and conjures memories of rural India. My favourite find was a small, unbroken medicine bottle at least a century old, complete with label: *La Miraculeuse*. My least favourite was a Vichy coin, showing a sheaf of corn (in truth, I was historically thrilled), its tin as light as a milk-bottle top in silver foil.

Fences were unknown in the Cévennes mountains until recently, due to flocks of goats or sheep having to have free access to pastures. Land boundaries were demarcated by flat slabs of stone thrust vertically into the ground, like teeth in gums: even boars can't root them out. Until a few years ago, the garden next to ours was a *potager*, or allotment, growing chick-peas, onions, leeks and a few rows of vines, owned and tilled for generations by the same Cévenol family. A drystone *bancèl* ran through the middle for most of its length, whose wall's configuration of grass-tufted stones I knew by heart, as our back-bedroom windows looked over it. Rusty old bed-ends and the iron hoops of wooden grape-tubs leaned against the walls, preventing it becoming too picturesque.

For my aforementioned friend, the popular *paysan* novelist Michel Jeury, it was the most typical Cévenol microcosm he knew, and he would walk up here from his own village just to look. The tussocked *bancèl* wall, unbrowbeaten by frost, became a locus of stability for me, helped by the nightingales which returned every spring from Africa to a ground-hugging nest near the chick-peas. They sang with enormous gusto right through the night and for most of the day. There was also a tombstone, where a young member of the family, back in the 1930s, felt thirsty while hoeing and grabbed what he thought was the water bottle, one of two identical dark-glassed flagons. The one he held to his lips contained treatment against mildew – sulphur mixed with Bordeaux mixture. Perfectly suitable for organic farming, it is lethal when swallowed. He died agonisingly and slowly, according to our neighbour – whose father was present to see the nephew's last moments. Thus even this modest patch held the ghosts of terrible dramas, the echoes of screams as well as present birdsong.

A few years back, the senior member of this family (the *doyen*) died. Having owned the *potager* and its neighbouring *mas* from time immemorial, with relevant papers dating back to the sixteenth century, the family sold it to a Norman couple looking for a drizzle-free holiday retreat. France's inheritance rules means this is not a rare occurrence even when certain family members are against, as our neighbour was: 'I've put years of my life into that soil,' he once told me. 'I kept it clean. No artificial fertiliser or insecticide!'

A digger arrived within days, puffing and snorting, an enormous crater appeared in the allotment and half the drystone wall vanished. The digger toppled over on the slope and broke a main branch of the cherry tree. The vehicle stayed there for a fortnight. The driver wasn't hurt, surprisingly, so I was delighted; perhaps it was the ghost of the poison victim. The Normans were reportedly irate about the damage to the cherry. The swimming pool emerged as though a slide had been pulled across to some underground laboratory. The nightingales never returned, and the only sound was the buzz of the pool's pump, like a perpetual, circling mosquito. Heat- and water-pumps have led otherwise placid neighbours to take an axe to them. I resisted, but I reminded my neighbours of this *fait divers*.

What I didn't mention was that those who own private swimming pools tend to miss out on the abundance of freshwater rivers in the area, entirely free and far more gladdening to the heart: secretive bathing places under alder and ash, complete with fleets of water striders at eye level, toe-nibbling fish and thermal shock, the currents swirling over blinding white alps of limestone, granite boulders rounded to a slipperiness, the bluish strata of schist. The local market town's huge and beautiful open-air pool is a decent back-up (and something of an anomaly, since the town itself is impoverished). The water is always cool and gurgles to the sides at ground level, so that the blinding tiles seem to translate effortlessly into the sparkling blue. Regulars there for some 20 years, we have come to know the couple who run it – former Olympic champions in whose presence my limbs feel like twigs. They nickname us *les Anglais Pélardons*, calling us 'the most Cévenol of all the English'.[1]

My mention of the axe must have made its mark, however, because attempts were made to muffle the pump's buzz. The nightingales stayed away.

Happily, the area immediately in front of the Normans' house is the previously mentioned *placette*; this is a grassed and beguiling oblong with a low wall at the far end to stop you plunging many metres into another garden below. On one side stood the modest medieval ruin known as l'Hôpital; it had survived countless centuries until the Normans bought the patch separately and demolished the relic, on safety grounds, in favour of a neatly paved terrace with historyless walls. The municipal green offers a reasonably flat area for *boules*, shade under its false-acacia trees for communal gatherings and a lovely view south for contemplation. I imagine it has served thus from the earliest years of a settlement here – perhaps more than a thousand years. When an actor friend and neighbour married a Congolese puppeteer on the green last year, accompanied by a barrel organ and accordion, they used the Normans' double flight of front steps or *perron* (an unusually grand feature for a *mas*) as a glove-puppet

---

[1] *Pélardon* being a goat's cheese unique to the Cévennes: grilled whole on toast with a dash of olive oil and a pinch of rosemary, served with a salad of tender greens, it is unbeatable.

theatre, with a blanket thrown over the wrought-iron railings. The owners, of course, were absent at the far end of this large country, it not being summer, and were blissfully ignorant.

When the original garden plot was sold along with the house, there was a tacit agreement between *vendeurs* and *acheteurs* that its resident tombstone should not be touched. As the latter have now secured all access to the former allotment, building solid stone walls and a large wooden gate – a very un-Cévenol tactic – I can't check whether the agreement has been honoured. If by carelessness or treachery they have removed it or covered it with earth, then I imagine some grander sort of supernatural revenge. Their attempts to privatise the communal space – or at least to make it look like theirs – with a slung hammock and bright yellow garden chairs for the three weeks they are here, along with a fresh, more permanent strategy consisting of rubber plants in heavy pots, invite an altogether more earthly revenge. I plan with other aggrieved neighbours to hold a *boules* championship there, preferably when the Normans are sunning themselves in their chairs. Will they lift their feet to allow the heavy balls free passage? Meanwhile, I have removed the plant-pots onto their personal steps and cricked my back.

They have all been returned onto the green, perhaps by gnomes. In certain circumstances, *Love thy neighbour* can be the most challenging ordinance of all.

10

A Flat Above the Café

After occasional trips to Paris or London, it's always a relief to take the train back to Nîmes and then the straight Roman road to the mountains, where almost everywhere you look there is no one, only trees and sky. You notice the quiet. Beyond the complex sonic mishmash of birdsong and leaf-rustle, punctuated by a horse's whinnies from the stables below, there is only the sigh of the wind. Apart from an indigo Iceland and much of Norway, Sweden and Scotland, a recent colour-coded noise-pollution map of Europe shows mere dabs and streaks of blue calm among the orange-yellow and red din, with almost nothing at all in England's desert-hued blare. One of the streaks corresponds almost exactly to the Cévennes National Park, just as the modest blue speck in southern Britain matches Dartmoor. I'm not sure any of this takes into account the throbbing interjections of passenger jets, or the village youth on their *mobilettes*, or the passing torture of exhaust-modified motorbikes out for a run in the country, or even the ripples of the pleasant if very loud village bell, its tolling unaltered since 1776, spreading along the valley to our hill. But it's a start.

Noise turned out to be a major issue once we'd moved for half of the year (weekdays in term-time) from the Cévennes to the centre of Nîmes, our nearest city. This was about 15 years ago. Our eldest was approaching lycée age and would have to weekly board in a secondary not known for its good results but for its pall of dope around the entrance (Jo had taught there, so this was more than hearsay). The children could walk to school, we could walk to work: my purely freelancing days were over, in the dour face of impoverishment – with my books resolutely refusing the vulgarity of bestsellerdom and prizes, against all authorial attempts to persuade them otherwise, my advances were now on a slippery slope of Cévenol gradient. My first 'French' novel, written of course in English, a thick tome set in a rapidly changing suburb of Paris in the 1960s but haunted by the Franco-Prussian War of 1870, got nowhere except in terms of critical appreciation. I write to surprise myself, among other pleasures, so taking the commercial road was out of the question.

We became, if not by any means well-off, financially stable; Jo teaches full-time in a Nîmes lycée. I began by lecturing part-time in the university and eventually landed a job as *prof d'anglais* in the city's state-funded art school, which lies conveniently a few doors up the street in a sternly classical eighteenth-century mansion built by a silk merchant: if I forget a book or document, I can set my students an exercise and be back before they've applied pen to paper. Films, theatre, bookshops and exhibitions are all a stroll away, as is the large covered market, a Rabelaisian delight with its olfactory mingling of fish, ripe cheese, trodden cabbage leaves, roasting chicken, candied fruit and coffee beans. This is where we do most of our food shopping. It is its own village. In fact, the entire centre of Nîmes, for all its bustle and size, is itself a village: I can never go out without bumping into several people I know, not all of them my students.

In the real village, our back door opens directly onto the rough cobblestones of the *calade*, scarcely trodden all day and mostly the haunt of birds or, now and again, clouds of butterflies. In Nîmes, our shared front door opens directly onto a narrow but busy street without the cushion of a pavement, unleashing sounds that seem to leap on you. The immediate area is becoming increasingly *populaire* (meaning working-class, not popular) and multi-ethnic. The discreet, bourgeois calm that greeted us on arrival is a thing of the past. At least for now.

We started out with a disadvantage in the flat itself. Despite the strait-laced appearance of the previous owners, both elderly, the interior resembled a West Berlin disco from the 1970s: the main room's ceiling alone consisted of red neon tubes artfully concealed above suspended trapezoids of yellow, purple and green polystyrene, and every wall had a different surface, from embossed stucco to fiendishly well-stuck cork. We spent most of the first sweltering summer dealing with this, receiving nine parking fines in the process and a broken wrist on my part when I fell off a ladder. Dismantling the two false ceilings, it then took me 60 hours on a scaffold to clean the revealed seventeenth-century ceiling beams and joists of their soot ('blackwash',

I called it). The main room now resembles, according to a visiting poet friend, the interior of a galleon. I hope not the gun deck, I joked.

The tons of rubble had to be carted down in buckets by Louis, the burliest of our village builders, to the lorry waiting round the corner. Despite his frequent moans, he brought a Cévenol determination to the project, lightened by his penchant for Belgian chocolates from the high-class *chocolaterie* immediately opposite. He had also fallen, as many others before and since, for Yasmine, *la très belle fille* (in his words) behind the counter. To watch his plaster-covered fingers pluck two or three pralines from the dainty box and deliver them into his huge mouth one after the other, surrounded by builder's mess and debris, was to come that much closer, perhaps, to the sweet heart of France's particularity.

When our building's co-owner, Monsieur Lafont – the local locksmith and blacksmith – met Louis for the first time, he took me aside and asked me what on earth did I think I was doing, hiring this fat country bumpkin? Recognising the gulf between city and country, I insisted that Louis was an excellent worker and that his fat was muscle, privately marvelling that M. Lafont, no stranger to a bellowing coarseness himself, could be so prejudicial in his judgements – even when racial issues were not involved.

Somehow, the place was ready to move into, despite the bare concrete floor and lack of furniture, by the time term started. A friend pointed out that, even if the jointly owned stairwell to our flat does resemble that of a decrepit nineteenth-century lodging house, like the murderous Laurent's in *Thérèse Raquin*, at least it puts burglars off.

Laying the wooden floor using a cut-price job-lot of pine planks helped the acoustics, as did the hanging of curtains, but anyway the noise two floors below was no more than a murmurous urban soundscape that was less than bothersome. From early November on, however, like many French towns, Nîmes fills its historic centre with piped music, emanating from small but powerful speakers, in a bid to encourage Christmas shopping. The yowls penetrate stone, double glazing and flesh. Once a year after midnight I don my blue overalls and fake municipal badge (*Ville de Nîmes* letterhead slipped into a Random House visitor-pass holder), take my apple hook (metal curtain rod with a coat-hanger taped to the end) and deal with the nearest wires. The chink in their armour is the connection between the main flex and the speaker's wire; a twist works better than a thrust, but the action has to be determined – you are working from some 12 feet below. The main challenge is to behave like a council worker and not like a nervous writer.

One year I neutralised the usual pair outside our flat, but a speaker extension had been added, close to my study window. I became so enraged by the cheerful, disembodied voice urging us to spend that I operated in civvies, in broad daylight, in front of mildly interested passers-by. The hollow metal pole, made up of two halves screwed together, snapped at the joint as I poked; it struck my head and fell on the pavement with a clatter just a whisker from a silver-haired old dear, whose concern for my health sounded clear in the sudden (relative) hush.

I am not alone. Opinion is divided between the city's two rival shopkeeper federations, each politically coloured. You can tell which camp certain shops belong to by the presence of silent speakers, at least during the festive season. It was a boutique owner who gave me the sabotage idea, miming it with a flick of her wrist.

Given my writerly sensitivity to sound, it was perhaps unwise of us to have bought a flat above a café. We had been reassured that the cathedral's proximity and the immediate area's ecclesiastical past meant that no café on the square could stay open late. And there were cultural precedents, mainly Parisian. Joseph Roth drank himself to death over (as well as in) the Café Tournon near the Luxembourg Gardens in the 1930s. Gene Kelly's Jerry Mulligan in the post-war MGM musical *An American in Paris* had a fine time above his Montmartre version, possibly because the film was made in California.

The Via Domitia runs a couple of minutes' walk from us: once connecting Rome and Iberia, with the status of a main motorway in classical times, it is now a tatty street known for pavement drug dealers. When we first arrived, these had an office in the café's corner table, the three gloomy derelicts having reportedly hung on through at least two changes of proprietor. But they were quiet, like the café as a whole, which served crêpes yet was dark and unappealing. This suited us, as both bedroom and study looked down on the threadbare awning.

Cities are rated these days by the vibrancy of their night life: luckily, Nîmes, a Protestant city, is a dead loss on this score, cramming all its late-night partying into its two ferias – the bullfighting festivals during which the sand of the great Roman arena runs with blood and the streets run with booze until dawn; most Nîmois flee the fun. After a few experimental seasons, so did we.

The café changed hands after a year or so. I was impressed by the new couple's energy. Henri was a muscular chef in his late thirties determined to make something of it, including decent food. 'We want the serious kind of customer.' One day we were startled by what sounded like a jet engine yards from my son's bedroom window: reviving the cellar kitchen also meant reviving the massive extractor fan on our roof, its brick housing quivering under the assault. Delicate negotiations resulted in minimal use at peak times, when Henri would all but suffocate, emerging from the kitchens below in a caul of sweat.

Arriving at 6 a.m., he worked without stopping until the last customer went: the aforementioned temperance zone around the cathedral turned out to be a folk memory. The problem wasn't the customers themselves, apart from the occasional British group finding life hilarious, very late, around a table. The café's success involved investment in wrought-iron tables and chairs, oak-limbed parasols as big as parachutes and massive ceramic plant jars, all so heavy they left drag marks on the flagstones. It took an hour for these toys to be tucked away in their box, crammed into every nook and cranny and pressed up against the plate glass, so it was well beyond midnight by the time the last iron paws were being scraped across the stone and nestled inside the house with a deep booming that the building's structure seemed to welcome all the way up to our attic.

Little Serge, with elephant ears, crooked shoulders and a cheeky-boy grin, was the aged *terrassier*, hired by several cafés to clear the decks at night. The furniture was too heavy to lift, he said. Henri listened to my complaints with a sympathy I was to test many times, unable to find the surface that proved it to be entirely false: he had only one interest behind the smiles, and that was not the welfare of writers.

Henri's wife, looking well rested behind the bar, suggested that my insomnia was due to psychological causes, and that I was projecting it onto the furniture. Henri cleverly took my side by railing against *terrassiers* in general and Serge in particular, showing me the claw marks on the municipal flagstones and the table legs loosened in their bolts. There was a brief improvement – at the apparent cost of Serge's back, which was made very clear to me whenever I passed him in the street. I would now manage to sleep before the cleaners came like a ransacking army at 5.30 a.m.

At dawn one morning, I saw black smoke coiling past our rear window. I phoned the fire brigade and alerted the tenant in the flat beneath ours, who fled with us in her nightgown onto the square. I went back in, coughing, to rescue my unfinished novel: the kind of idiocy that might have made the UK tabloids (or at least the qualities, hopefully) if I had died as a result. The fire engines took 20 minutes to come. By the time Henri arrived, oddly late for once, the gas-masked firemen had filled his cellar kitchen with foam. His wife was in tears, but two months later he had state-of-the-art units mostly paid for by the insurance. He blamed a defective chip-maker.

Then, having told me life wasn't just about work, Henri decided to stay open on Sundays. The café had mutated into a café-restaurant, but the chef was no longer Henri: he was now generally hunched outside, panda-eyed and unshaven, holding forth mysteriously often to a table of attractive young women, who were never the same. Perhaps, I rather meanly thought, they operate in shifts.

The late-night timpani of shifted furniture continued. Someone mentioned defence as the best line of attack. Lining the walls with egg boxes was one option. Inspired by Proust's example, I also considered cork. The most serious incursions, however, were on the back of draughts around our bedroom's tall double windows. One morning saw my younger son and me walking back from the glazier behind Nîmes station at either end of two very long sheets of glass. A newspaper was draped on top to signal to passers-by that the transparent space between us was not walk-through. I kept imagining a scene from one of those comic French films from the mid-century, starring Louis de Funès or Jacques Tati and full of elaborate pratfalls.

The double-glazing kit (a few plastic strips to hold the glass) looked easy, but was not. I finished it off with cork-lined inner shutters clamped tight each night against the frames. This triple sealant muffled the street effects, but was mysteriously ignored by both Serge's efforts and the bass thudding from cars waiting for the lights with their windows down, their drivers eager to share their taste in rock, reggae or shababi with the entire slumbering *quartier*.

Occasionally in the early hours I was driven to opening our bedroom window and yelling down at Serge, who would give an apologetic wave and carry stuff in surgically for a few nights. He had a tendency to divide his task into several parts, like a long play, the intermissions spent alone in the bar. Just when we were drifting off, the next act would start with a boom or a rasp in which I could actually judge the alcohol level.

One night, well after one o'clock, I heard Henri's voice over the thumps. I cracked completely and stormed into the café in my dressing gown – or rather, squeezed my way over stacked chairs, to grab a bottle off the counter and wave it about. Henri's nervous shrug dissatisfied me. Jerry Mulligan would have danced and sung, and the two men would have joined in; instead, I pushed over one of the stacks, which just missed Serge. Like the silver-haired old dear just missed by the pole, he didn't tell me off but, to my confusion, looked at his boss, spread his hands and in a soft voice said *le monsieur* was quite right: the furniture was far too heavy.

Eventually I phoned the city's Service Hygiène, whose '*lutte contre les nuisances sonores*' takes top place in its list of aims. As the others include *dératisation* and the salubrity of food, Henri was already known to the service. Monsieur Baudry promised to pay the premises a visit that very week.

Despite my grumblings and recent tantrum, Henri remained friendly. He wanted to pull out of the long-term lease, which he couldn't default on without being sued by the landlord (M. Roger, our co-proprietor), and wanted to keep me on side in case I told prospective tenants that the spot was commercially doomed. Given I was desperate for him to leave, I was more likely to tell them it was a goldmine. Meanwhile, in a bid to attract custom, he had festooned the area with yet larger blackboards, placards full of exclamation marks and at least three more tables: holes drilled into the slabs had finally resulted in victory for the vast parasols in their frequent battle with the mistral. It reminded me of a military camp, dug in for the foreseeable future. I was, I suppose, the enemy sapper. His son had joined him, barely out of his teens, and didn't make a point of being friendly. Henri's wife was nowhere to be seen, these days. 'She's studying for a degree,' I was told. But not in Nîmes.

I had allies. The *police municipale* came along and re-established the precise limits – beyond which Henri's paraphernalia had lately crept – with a white line and a warning. They also told him to leave a corridor through the maze of tables for hapless pedestrians. Monsieur Baudry phoned me and said that he had paid his visit and had suggested rubber wheels. The wheels never materialised and our insomnia grew worse as little

Serge, still the official *terrassier*, deteriorated in health and enthusiasm. Meanwhile, the smell of reused fat had grappled any lingering aniseed whiffs of pastis to the ground. I phoned the Service Hygiène again.

This time, Monsieur Baudry brought along a computer with decibel-recording software and a powerful microphone. The latter was set up discreetly in our bedroom, aiming through the open window. Henri had been forewarned, as was his right, but not told when. The computer's screen showed a graph with a red line jaggedly rising and falling to the noises beyond our bedroom window, tracing an Alpine range. Cars were the Mont Blanc, building up to a lofty peak as they swished past: but they don't swish, that is an illusion fostered by smooth-talking progress. Cars lay waste our ears, according to the machine. The staccato of high-heeled shoes punched the air, voices held the lower slopes.

The aim was to snare the decibel-smashing, post-midnight drag of the café furniture, and to show Henri that he was breaking the law. Baudry was a nuclear physicist by training, he told me, had spent years in a nuclear power station. A balance had to be kept between entertainment and the needs of residents. Sleep, he said, is every citizen's right. He shook my hand and said he would be back in three days.

The furniture that night was moved silently, balletically, as if by elves. I had caught Henri looking up at our open window and had foolishly ducked out of sight, wondering if the microphone on its stand was visible. As the recording straddled a weekend, we could take refuge in the Cévennes. We returned on Sunday evening for the machine's last night and once again the furniture was elf-carried. I gave up hope. When Monsieur Baudry reappeared late Monday afternoon, I told him about the elves. He laughed, fiddled with the computer and compressed the three-day record into a cartoon hospital temperature chart, through which he slowly scrolled.

'Ah, *voilà*,' he said. One of the peaks punctured the limit. He stretched the trace like elastic, examined it as a doctor would a scan, noted precisely when it had happened the previous night, and nodded. I vaguely recalled a drunken *gaillard* striking a bollard with something metal, but kept quiet. 'That's it,' he went on. 'That's all we need.' I asked him if he was sure it was the clearing of the *terrasse*.

He traced the summits with his finger.

'Without any doubt,' he said, in the assured way of a French nuclear physicist.

Henri appeared in court for disturbing the peace, and claimed the timing was all wrong, but before the considerable fine was upheld at appeal, he moved.

Soon after, in the top-floor café-restaurant of the city's swish médiatheque, I was admiring the view of the Maison Carrée below, when Henri's son loomed up to my table in creamy waiter's uniform.

We were equally startled, but recovered our poise. He was polite. His father had landed on his feet in this prestigious place as principal chef.

My coffee, when eventually it arrived, tasted a touch bitter.

All that Rough Music

A colleague at the art school took me aside one day. 'I've made a video. Could you do a voice-over? *J'ai besoin d'un accent anglais.*' Videos in the context of the École Superieure des Beaux Arts usually involve protracted, repetitive scenes of puzzling import, but Frédérique assured me that this was just 'a home thing for a local cycling website. A few extracts from Robert Louis Stevenson.'

The elliptical nature of his reference to *Travels with a Donkey in the Cévennes* was telling: Stevenson's account of his twelve-day trek with the overburdened and intractable donkey, Modestine, through the wildest stretch of France is embedded in local mythology. This was true when Richard Holmes tramped the same route in 1964 and evocatively recounted it 20 years later in *Footsteps*; it is even more so now. Apart from a choice of translations, the 120-mile voyage exists as comic book, theatre show, a TV series, a dedicated Topoguide for hikers (which scolds the ex-Calvinist for overlooking the Catholic masterpieces on the way) and an association developing the tourist potential of *le Chemin de Stevenson GR70.*

René and Christine, old friends of ours, make a precarious living from hiring out donkeys up near Florac, sending their clients off with their own Modestines – 'docile and intelligent', they claim. The overnight stays along the way are prearranged, which seems to defeat the object, but wild camping (which Stevenson fell back on nervously) is technically illegal in France. I presumed that our friends' clients would be largely my compatriots. 'No,' said René, 'mainly German and Dutch. It just takes one article in a magazine, and *c'est l'effet boule de neige*. And they all know *Treasure Island*.' At least, I suggested, those Brits who do come are probably ready to rough it a little in the spirit of the original. '*Mais non*,' came the laughing reply from Christine. Apparently, the British prefer organised tour groups, whose agents are demanding. Last year, two came from London to inspect the *hébergement* for a group of 20; they fussed that some places were more primitive than others, that all the overnights had to be of the same standard. They then insisted, with months still to go, and displaying a disarming ignorance of Cévenol ways, that the whole circuit had to be booked within two days flat, or they would pull out. Which they did, by now so far from the spirit of the original that they might as well have been planning a package tour to Majorca.

I shook my head in familiar shame: Brits in general are the least popular with gîte-owners, too, tending to over-imbibe and jape around. Anecdotes abound. After one party had left the smart house in question a wreck from a birthday weekend, with all the garden furniture in the pool, the young Englishman in charge responded to the complaints with a fat cheque. '*Les Anglais* seem to be rich, but *sans politesse*,' was our friend's comment. And this was before Brexit.

I told René and Christine that my own Stevensonian voyage in the drought year of 1976 was conducted on an even more docile Puch 1.5 HP moped: kickstarted with the pedal, cruising at 30mph, sounding like a wasp caught in the ear, it similarly took me to unplanned places inside myself as I buzzed between poplars and plane trees down long French country roads, the reassuring road signs still in concrete and blue-lettered enamel, my face masked in dark-brown dust.

The extracts I had to record for Frédérique were among my best loved: the artless finesse of the originals came through in translation. I didn't tell him that I tend to avoid many stretches of the famous route, preferring solitude; according to Laurence Sterne, solitude enables the mind to 'lean upon itself' and be strengthened. On any other Cévenol path you scarcely meet a soul apart from the odd shepherd and his tintinnabulary flock, with the occasional scrambler bike to shake your fist at through a squall of exhaust fumes and noise.

Things have changed since Holmes's day, let alone Stevenson's: the future of these beleaguered hills is in eco-tourism – with RLS, having pioneered 'coming down off the feather-bed of civilization', showing the way. However, his route is partly guesswork: the descriptions in *Travels* are rarely detailed enough for anyone to know for certain if the path is the genuine article. In 1878, the roads would have been rough and unpaved where they are now slick with tarmac: if they snake through the hills in just the same often precipitous manner, they are made hopelessly unsuitable for pedestrians by the world of cars. The *chemin de Stevenson* is an inevitable compromise. Deviations are necessary. Given that his journey was as much of the soul as the body, this only matters to literary groupies, but it also triggers a wider regret.

Take the last day's march, between the remote village of Saint-Étienne-Vallée-Française and Stevenson's endpoint in Saint-Jean-du-Gard – a mere 20 minutes from our own village. His final 'long descent' to Saint-Jean followed 'a long and steep ascent' to the high col de Saint-Pierre, where he and Modestine ate their last and moonlit snack together. In 1994, as recounted in his equally haunting *To Travel Hopefully*, a grief-stricken Christopher Rush and his donkey found the climb 'the rockiest and steepest yet of the entire journey' (but the endeavour, as for the consumptive and lovelorn Stevenson, was a healing one).

A dented, semi-legible sign on the col itself, the meeting place for every wind going, is currently the only visible clue: *Chem . . . venson*. Despite superb views (arriving at dusk, our tired pilgrim could only see 'the yawning valley, gulfed in blackness ... like a hole in created nature at my feet'), the col has lost its vibes thanks to a speeding D road. The latter, in its former ponderous and dusty guise, was clearly RLS's actual route down off the top. This is where the regret comes in – for what progress has demanded that we sacrifice.

Fortunately, the only way he could have climbed up from Saint-Étienne is by the present path, which switches from forester's track to a thin trail authentically matted by embedded stones. On our latest walk there a few weeks ago, I took my battered 1914 copy of *Travels* and read the relevant passages aloud to Jo. On Stevenson's climb to the col he was shadowed by an empty carriage, the driver convinced he was a pedlar; on the descent to Saint-Jean he 'met no one but a carter, visible afar off by the glint of the moon on his extinguished lantern', a detail anticipating *Treasure Island*'s terrifying opening chapters (which, when I read them as a boy, reached subliminal depths and stayed put). We met no one at all in the wintry sunlight.

Saint-Étienne, a huddle of stone houses under a medieval chateau, must have changed little in appearance, although like all such places it has, in fact, changed utterly. Half the buildings have the artificial-coma look of summer residences, there are home-made signs pointing to various craft ateliers, and it doesn't smell of dung or imperfect drainage (as rural French villages still did, I remember, in the 1960s, and as ours did when we first arrived). The sole residents visible were a few teenagers kicking a football in the road. The wonky little church was open and much of its mouldering interior would have been recognised by Stevenson, as would the tiny square that its off-centre clock stared down upon, where we ate our sandwiches.

The place always reminds me of another ramshackle village on Stevenson's route: Le Bleymard lies at the foot of towering Mont Lozère. Many years ago we would holiday there off-season to hike through the heather. We were chiefly attracted to it because, somewhere in the forest around Bleymard, Stevenson famously slept out 'under the pines' in his self-devised sleeping bag. His account of this 'new pleasure' (if less confessional than in his travel notebook) memorably weaves physical sensation and metaphysical speculation to the whiffs of a cigarette under the stars. Like those to whom Holmes had talked thirty-odd years earlier, the garage man in Bleymard knew all about the long-haired author. When I mentioned 'that donkey' he said, 'Ah! Modestine!' and laughed as if at some personal recollection. I almost asked if he had met them. 'Do you have any idea where he actually slept out?' Glancing around at the fir-clad slopes, he shook his head. 'No one does. I slept out myself as a boy, *dans la nature*. It's magic,' he added, through the petrol fumes.

This encounter already seems many leagues back in time. I thought of it as we puffed back up to the col recently, and of Holmes's predecessor, J. A. Hammerton, who found Bleymard 'mean and featureless' in 1903. Paying his homage by bicycle rather than on foot, he occasionally met those who had crossed paths with the young Scot; the pastor in Pont de Montvert even produced a glum-looking photo of Clarisse, the auberge waitress so lingeringly described in *Travels*. Hammerton's book, *In the Track of R. L. Stevenson and*

Elsewhere, makes for fascinating reading: he likewise regrets the changes that have occurred over 25 years, yet in 1903 the peasantry still wear wooden *sabots* and speak in dialect, the women are all in black, the floors are earthen, the village streets are 'filth-sodden' and stink of the byre (and are often jammed by sheep), snatches of song can be heard, there is work in the fields and orchards, and everyone argues and drinks too much.

Traces of this deep rurality were still intact in 1964, when Holmes set out – as they were to a certain extent in 1990, when we came to live here. The dialect, for instance: there were three old men who would occasionally sit on the stone bench in front of the café, chatting in Occitan. I distinctly recall the last time I heard them; only two were left, and it was up on the path near our house. A knot of the past that soon slipped and let all that rough music go, and I'm not sure anyone noticed.

With the help of mobile phone masts and EU rules, the Cévennes are cleaned up, less eccentrically particular – easier on the Dutch, one might say. The jobs are as few as the songs, our *département* being one of the poorest in France. A continuing influx of back-to-the-earthers has scarcely made up for the chronic exodus to the urbs, already started in Stevenson's time, and now biblical drought is promised from climate change. Not coming down off that feather-bed has been a costly business, I reflected, as we reached the tarmac and our ever-docile car.

12

Erudition

We were sitting in our favourite café in our favourite village. Not our own village, but another huddle of houses in the neighbouring commune: under four miles as the crow flies, if the crow doesn't mind gaining altitude fast, but 20 minutes by car; the road meanders severely as it climbs through chestnut and beech woods. The village is not limestone like ours but granite. The air is different, as if you're suddenly in an Alpine resort. The vegetation plays along with this illusion: a lot of pines and spruce in dark green swathes on the higher slopes, and tumbling streams among the great boulders, and the odd solitary eagle eyeing us from the level of the peaks. We never considered living there because there'd been no school for years, and a lot of the houses are uninhabited most of the year. The second-homers arrived in the 1960s from Germany, Holland and Belgium. These early adventurers are now elderly or worse, but their children and grandchildren are not interested in a remote, frequently chilly sector of the French South. So the ancient houses are empty, and often unsellable.

The café's owners greet us warmly. The place is quiet tonight. We spot Cédric's shaved head in the brownish gloam. We have walked up to the village on sandy paths through the woods, leaving the car as usual where the tarmac runs out just above the col. It's our favourite shortish walk, with several minor alternatives, and lasts about three hours there and back; this time we decided to climb a little further into the village itself and have a beer before the downhill return. We met Cédric in his battered little Renault just before the village: he is a fashion designer whose annual summer *défilé* takes place high up in the pasture of a huge old farmhouse where he now lives alone, renting a few rooms from the venerable lady still running the place: the parade is an essential date in the local calendar. Over the years he has moved from extravagant commissions, to which he gives his own even wilder and inimitable touch in unexpected materials, to *prêt-à-porter*. He now finds this boring, he tells us, with a wink, so this year's parade will be back to form, with jackets of lace, silk shirts almost as long as robes, roomy trousers in primary colours and shimmering silvery dresses struggling to be tamed in the wind that always pours over the lonely peak on the big day.

'See you in the café,' he said.

Next to him at the bar is an enthusiastic man in his late thirties with a close-cut beard, whom I vaguely recognise. We talk about beech martens; about the nocturnal, black-spotted, mysterious *genettes*; and whether the slender snakes in the rivers are dangerous – a subject which particularly exercises Jo. The man's name is Léon. He appears to be an expert on wildlife: he knows, for instance, that the cat-sized genet is neither feline nor vulpine but from a distinct family, the viverrids. 'And it is very smelly,' he adds. The only specimen I have seen was dead and in a photo, sent to me by a friend who found the cadaver near his house in the Montagne Noir. It looked like a fantasy creature stitched together from commoner species, with a fox's nose.

Léon turns out to be a member of the main tribe in the village, rivals to our own main tribe 'down below', as he pointedly puts it. He unpacks the family surname, its etymology, its linguistic variants. 'It derives from Latin *villanus*,' he says. 'Not a thief originally, but the servant that came with the villa you bought. Chained to it, like a dog. A slave, really. Nothing but trouble. The lowest of the low. Villains, that's us.'

'Villein,' I proffer, 'in English. A kind of serf.'

'In fact,' Cédric points out, 'English is mostly French.'

'Guillaume le Conquérant,' the other explains. There then follows an expert analysis, not only of William the Conqueror's brutality (psychologically deriving from his bastard origins), but of the Battle of Hastings and its ruthless aftermath. Very few people in France have even heard of Hastings: the date 1066 strikes no chords.

'Yes, I've always thought of him as a psychopath,' I break in, turning the hand wheel on the vintage peanut dispenser, holding the little plastic plate to catch my 20 centimes-worth.

'No,' says Léon, in apparent teacher mode, 'he wasn't. That's the point.'

He then embarks on the complexity of noble blood-ties that meandered towards the Hundred Years War, the

coldly fanatical Henry V, and the Battle of Agincourt –
or Azencourt, as the French more accurately call it,
for whom this slaughter is a mere detail in that ghastly
conflict, and frequently less than that: a blank. Again,
and ever surprisingly, Léon treats us to a succinct
description of the battle itself, miming the high angle at
which the English longbowmen released their arrows
to swoop down from the arc into the flower of French
chivalry. The bar's beamed ceiling takes their imagined
impact with customary imperturbability. Up to 10,000
men died or were wounded in an ear-splitting orgy of
killing: infamously, many of the French were slain after
being taken prisoner (on Henry's panicked orders). It
may all have been over in an hour. I only know this
because I wrote and presented a programme for the
600th anniversary on BBC Radio Three, walking about
in the vast field's aptly glutinous mud as I played the
expert. But I avoid mentioning this to Léon: he seems
to know more about the battle, or at least my country's
royal genealogy, than I do. I don't fancy being rumbled
as an ignoramus *britannique* on my own historical
territory.

He cradles his Pelforth beer and dwells on Jeanne
d'Arc: did we know that she didn't burn at all but
was rescued? 'And now appears as Marine Le Pen,'
I comment, realising too late that there are several
regulars within earshot, half-hidden in the shadows.
But no one reacts. Survival of martyrs, especially
this freakish martyr – a demure teenage shepherdess
leading the battered French to victory in polished steel

armour – is an old favourite of conspiracy theorists, but Léon begins another trail that sounds much more scholarly than the usual wishful thinking. As ever, I am willing to entertain the idea that she was smuggled away.

'Perhaps it was the same angels,' I suggest, 'who guarded the Camisards a couple of centuries later.'

'We all need our angels,' says Cédric, pulling a face. He is struggling somewhat with high fashion in the rural wastes.

As we pick through our remaining ration of peanuts, contemplating the hike back, Léon tells us that Louis XIV's dragoons were stationed in the village for 40 years, keeping an eye on those filthy Prots: their billet was the huge, four-square building at the bottom of the lane (strikingly similar to the one yards from our own house called *Le Fort*, which once played the same role).

I know the building, I tell Léon: it's next door to the modest stone barn where my actor friend Jacques and two musicians performed the shepherd chapter in *Ulverton* three nights running – in French, naturally. The chapter concerns the return of a villager from Cromwell's wars in Ireland, straight into the hard new puritan world where festivities are banned. On the first night, we had to drag in more benches and were still turning people away. Over the years of its haphazard touring, some locals have seen it nine or ten times, and the word gets round. Afterwards, for each of the three nights, we all retired to this very café, and its four walls rang to the village veterans remembering – not always word-perfectly, not always in tune – the old songs in Occitan as well as French, supplemented by our musicians. Life doesn't get much better, I remember thinking over my beer. I don't mention any of this to Léon, who is embarked on a philosophical threnody concerning the inability of human beings to live together peacefully.

Dusk is falling on memories and the present moment alike, and we have to head back or we'll find ourselves stumbling along under a veiled half-moon. I shake Léon's hand. 'Are you, by any chance, a history teacher?' 'Oh no,' he laughs, 'I'm just a local dolt.' Cédric hopes to see us at the fashion parade in a fortnight.

We're weary by the time we reach the car, and decide to go for a pizza in our other neighbouring commune, where the old man on the bench once recounted the midday flood of silk-workers filling the very long and narrow high street. Hunger turns the pizza delicious. Crossing the square, we bump into Émil, the mayor of our favourite village, who also runs the Tabac in this one. We tell him about our encounter in the café, how impressed we were by the lecture on English history. Maybe Léon studied history at university? Émil shakes his head under its straggly mop of grey hair. '*Un érudit,*' he says. '*Tout simplement.*' His eyes glance up at the surrounding hills. '*Il y en a quelques-uns ici, quand même!*'

A scholar. A pure scholar. Not quite Arnold's scholar gypsy, more Hardy's Jude the Obscure. This romantic comparison is slightly dented at a birthday party a few days later, when I make further enquiries of an old friend born in Léon's village. Vincent runs a carpentry shop there with his identical twin: while the latter married a local girl and has several children, Vincent married Simon, a social worker from the north, back in the days when being anything other than straight or chaste in these stern, remote hills was unimaginable. It caused a stir, before the sawdust settled and work resumed as before – including my study's double windows in chestnut wood.

'Ah yes, Léon,' says Vincent, his laconic demeanour aided by a strong, slow-paced Cévenol accent. '*L'intellectuel.*'

'Yes, but self-taught.'

Vincent shrugs. 'His parents were teachers. His grandmother was head of the village school, she taught several generations of us.'

I felt secretly disappointed. Jude the Not-So-Obscure. 'Still,' I pointed out, 'his knowledge of English history was astonishing.'

Vincent paused a moment and then tapped his head, with his customary hint of a smile. 'Well, he's got a lot of the grey stuff up here. A bright spark, all right. *Un petit futé.*'

Did I detect, not only a whiff of derision, but a touch of envy?

Émil's remark about there being quite a few *érudits* in these lonely mountains had suggested that my surprise was misplaced. The Huguenots brought with them a respect for the word and an eye for business (they specialised in silk and leather). Books, faith, learning and graft. Shepherds crouched over their pocket Bibles. Fervent farmhands illuminated by the Scriptures. Protestant rebels being read to in their hideouts, their caves. Erudition slowly accreting through oral tradition as much as books. They were also suspicious of the image – a dislike fiercer among Calvinists than Lutherans, most of whom disapproved of burning paintings, punching out stained glass and decapitating statues. Sadly, British Puritanism, like Cévenol Puritanism, was largely Calvinist, and destroyed roughly nine-tenths of the country's medieval heritage before going off to colonise America in a spirit of manifest destiny.

When we first arrived, we frequently passed a shepherdess whose flock browsed the margins of the oxbow. She spent the long hours outside reading poems and writing her own in a notebook. But she was an import, originally from Paris.

Léon is homebred. He belongs in a long line. But might he be among the last? Will his successors read at all, or even listen?

A nineteenth-century lithograph I bought for a couple of euros in a flea market, entitled *Cévenoles Lisant la Bible*, shows three generations of women on benches before a glowing hearth, the youngest in her teens reciting the Holy Book to the others. The old dame in a shawl looks rapt, the other seems a little sleepy after a hard day. Around here it's the women who have always run the family accounts, as well as working in the fields. Up until recently, anyway: over the last few years the general physical wiriness has been replaced by a growing plumpness and even obesity.

In the village with the never-ending high street, where we stand talking to Émil, there's been a remarkable influx of 'les hippies', a new generation of back-to-earthers who are more radically dressed than their predecessors, including straightforward medieval garb for one group – all cloaks, tunics and bodices. And they are slim, even bony in some cases, the tattoos crossing sharp clavicles or swirling over pencil-thin wrists. Many are vegans.

A knowledgeable inhabitant told me, as we stood in the river's welcome chill a week ago, that the hippies only appear so numerous in the village because they walk everywhere, their children tumbling about in the streets as in old times; the locals, she informed me, 'are always in their cars, and their kids inside the house playing video games'. This seems a bewilderingly long way from the Calvinist trio wrapping up their gruelling day in the fields with a few holy words, yet we are talking about not much more than three generations: the rocks, trees and streams are the same, of course, but so are most of the houses.

A traditional streak of truculence, rebellion or even anti-pagan puritanism might have been present, however, when earlier in the year a group of these villagers smashed up and torched seven of the painted hippy vans next to the long-closed silkworm factory, where the more marginal elements are camped and play their bongos. 'We all know who they are, but that's where it stops,' said my informant. 'The police are locals too, after all. They go hunting together.'

I avoid mentioning the incident to Émil, who has enough to worry about in the neighbouring commune. 'By the way,' he adds as we bid each other goodbye, 'my grandson is obsessed with Sir Walter Scott.'

'Really?'

'He loves it. I'm reading it to him each night. Ivanhoe, Richard Coeur de Lion, Rob Roy . . .'

'Robin des Bois,' I quickly slip in, again nervous that I might be rumbled.

'Yes, he knows them all! And Quentin Durward, of course!'

As if, as an *érudit britannique*, I should know all about Durward, too. '*Bien sûr*,' I echo, grinning. 'How old is your grandson?'

'Four,' says Émil.

13

A Local Custom

The slopes of the southern Cévennes are mostly dark green with holm oak, but the patches of deciduous oak, along with spreads of chestnut, beech, mulberry and ash, mark the autumn with bright yellow streaks. So do the hunters in their equally bright but considerably less attractive jackets – these are now compulsory, in an attempt to reduce accidents. When an ex-lycée pupil of Jo's was shot dead last year while out walking on a public path with his girlfriend, there was no question of restricting the sport: instead, it was suggested that high-visibility garb should spread to all users of the countryside, from mushroom pickers to hikers, as a prerequisite for being insured.

On average, two or three non-hunters are shot dead or maimed each year. The toll on participants, however, is high enough to keep them kitted out as blots on the landscape. This might have saved Billy Pilgrim's father in Vonnegut's *Slaughterhouse-Five*, but not Hautot père in Maupassant's story *Hautot père et fils*, who made the common mistake of dropping his gun to seize the dead partridge. When we first came to live here in 1990, hunters were mostly dressed from head to foot in military camouflage, presumably in the hope that the boars, foxes, deer and game birds wouldn't spot them. They were certainly camouflaged from their companions. As there was no legal requirement to plant warning signs back then ('*Attention: Chasse en cours*'), or post sentries with their shotguns broken and open along the edges of the hunt's territory, it was easy to find yourself stumbling into a phalanx of armed men and their hyperactive dogs.

This happened to us in our first month in France, when we were renting the old olive mill in the oxbow: the latter, being a near-island, was perfect for hunting. It might as well have been a giant sack (which it somewhat resembles from the air), bulging with quarry. Its population of wild boars had been so decimated, however, that nobody now bothered to come. My informant was Raoul, the owner of our nearest hardware shop, where I was buying a ladder. 'Oh,' I found myself saying, 'only a couple of days ago I saw a big fat boar followed by about six little ones. It was very touching.'

The next day, as Jo had dolefully predicted on my return, we walked a hundred yards from our gate and straight into the middle of a hunt, led by Raoul. He suggested we turn round and go back home. I began to babble about our rights. A gunshot and excited shouts decided us. We trotted back as fast as we could, pursued by the pretty tinklings of the dogs' neck-bells, which was to become a familiarly sinister sound over the years. A few weeks later, walking the other side of the river in the private but beguiling woods of a posh chateau, a deafening blast brought leaves pattering gently on our heads. A shot across the bows, if ever there was one. We scuttled off, albeit whistling loudly, as obedient as the pre-Revolution peasantry.

Any residual sympathy for hunters as bearers of rural tradition is apt to be diluted by the sight of their bellies and the menacing, bumper-heavy four-by-fours. Until the recent past, sinewy hunting teams would set off at dawn and walk many miles to find their quarry, then return with 70-odd kilos of boar slung between them. Their rifles were less powerful. Rumours now abound of guns smuggled in from Russia whose particularly penetrating bullets can strike from over two miles away; worse, that there are still a few semi-psychotic diehards who use strictly illegal dum-dum bullets. I'm assuming the latter is the rural equivalent of an urban legend.

Several years ago, I wrote a thriller set in the Cévennes. It features Jean-Luc, a jobbing gardener and disturbed loner who recalls his father telling him of wartime hunts, including a double kill. Maupassant was my chief inspiration in this section: many of his 'woodcock' stories display an ambivalent attitude to the sport. One of his narrators admits to being 'passionately fond of shooting, and the sight of the bleeding animal, with the blood on its feathers and on my hands, affects my heart so, as almost to make it stop'. I forced myself to enter a similar mind-set: 'There's a panting and a snorting and it's two big beasts followed by three little ones crossing the field in a line … He lifts his gun and aims at the leader's flank just in front of the groin and he fires and the boar squeals and stumbles … and then it's the second running into the notch of his sights . . .' He misses the second and hits one of the piglets instead.

Writing it, I experienced a thrill; I was there, I was sighting it, the target was down. This was not just the writer's imagination at work, however: as a twenty-year-old, soon after my parents left Cameroon, I went shooting in the Cairngorms with members of the Likomba Golf Club, an eclectic group of Cameroonians and ex-pats, one of whom was a strapping Scottish plantation owner called Angus who had survived everything equatorial Africa had thrown at him; he suggested we go hunting over his ancestral moors as a break from the fairways.

Despite almost blowing my foot off when climbing a gate (an early lesson in the importance of the safety catch), my .22 bagged three hares. Angus said I was a natural shot. At school I was mediocre at every sport except for target practice in the Cadet Corps, when I somehow kept puckering the bull's eye without really thinking about it. Those two days in Scotland were some of the most thrilling of my life.

This doesn't mean that I approve of our local hunts, but I am uncomfortably aware of the attraction. I once joined in, albeit unarmed, for research purposes. Again, as we scanned the rosemary-scented underbrush and the steep slopes – my companion, a chatty veteran, happy to talk of the days when hunts were authentic slogs – my eyes seemed to acquire new lenses. Every leaf stood out, the shadows translated into meaning, the landscape somehow crawling up my legs into my dutifully thumping heart. The distant brass horn blared, one of the weirdest sounds I know, full of ancient, pre-musical echoes. I found myself being envious of my companion's slim, beautifully polished rifle. What was happening to me? I was identifying with the opposition, as every good novelist has to. Or was I discovering my atavistic roots, the lees of evolutionary change? As Barry Lopez puts it in *Arctic Dreams*, 'To hunt means to have the land around you like clothing.' You engage in a 'nonrational, nonlinear comprehension of events', similar to dreaming.

Lopez is talking about the Inuit, aboriginal hunters with an entirely different approach to Nature: they are not separated from it and from its animals, as we are. When I approached my first struck hare on the Scottish moorland, it looked straight into my eyes with a perplexed scrutiny that has haunted me existentially ever since. Our fates were intimately bound: its consciousness, filled with pain, recognised that as much as I did, but in a way that would never register on any of the rational instruments by which we measure our lives and environments and believe ourselves monarchs of the planet.

Nothing so grandiose (or philosophically tolerant) affects me when I pass a four-by-four in front of the village café of a Saturday afternoon, the bonnet smothered by a bloodied corpse, the boar's tongue lolling, pastis sugaring the air. There are at least two rumoured cases of local murders that have been disguised as hunting accidents, one involving a German hippy back in the 1980s who was about to elope with one of the daughters of the main village clan. The discovery more recently of a victim peppered by shot on the gravel shores of a nearby river was put down to a family row. Our burly neighbour, approaching 70, who was banned for life from keeping a rifle or hunting dogs, again speeds off every day to check his kennels. His own brother, a shepherd, told me he was left deaf in one ear after a dispute over a kill had resulted in a filial bullet buzzing past his temple.

A blind eye is being turned not because many gendarmes are also hunters, but because, when it comes to *sangliers* (as the right wing say of *fonctionnaires*), 'there are too many'. They dig up vineyards, maize fields and gardens. This year, a year of drought, they have rotavated my flower-beds, demolished my drystone walls and exposed my modest pond as not much more than a muddy puddle, leaving tell-tale traces of cloven hoofs. To them, my lovingly crafted feature is a water-hole to be wallowed in, an outside *estaminet* that they visit every evening during this exaggeratedly dry summer weather in a din of snorts and grunts, levering out boulders and tossing aside my feeble chicken-wire protection, helping themselves to nibbles in the form of iris and crocus bulbs, seemingly intent on reducing my garden to a simulacrum of Passchendaele – or the average pig-farm. I have slung New Age bells and pissed next to the pond (they have a remarkable sense of smell), to only brief avail.

In desperation last week I sought the advice of our burly hunter neighbour of the volatile temperament. His equally burly wife answered the door and put it succinctly: no compost heap, no pond, no watering in the evening. She also informed me that they're rooting out the fat white grubs (beetle larvae) that live in compost and underground, not the bulbs themselves. (That is probably a benefit, if the beetle is a vine weevil or the loud-buzzing cockchafer.) And try mothballs. She had seen seven *sangliers* trotting brazenly along the lane: mum and the fattening kids.

That night, I heard a couple of gunshots above the garden. For the first time ever, I hoped it was our neighbour, helping me out. As a friend put it the other day, only half-jokingly: 'Hunters have become a public service!'

Although it is a fact that boars have never been so bold and numerous, I did open the front door years ago to find a fully grown specimen staring at me balefully over its tusks. With countless hectares of brush and forest all around us, and rugged valley after rugged valley to the north, with two hundred miles of uplands – the entire Massif Central – between us and the Loire basin, it is hardly surprising if Nature fails to distinguish the tame from the wild.

Wicked tongues suggest that the animals have been deliberately interbred with the more fertile domestic pig to turn hunting from pastime into necessity. I doubt this is quite true – there has always been natural interbreeding, and the local specimens look fairly fearsome, quite able to eviscerate a dog: just recently, returning through woods from a neighbouring party, we found two friends crouched behind their car, unpicking thorns from their respective skirts. 'We heard a *sanglier*,' one panted, between giggles, 'and ran for cover, straight into the brambles. It followed us. It was enormous!' The other half-shrieked, half-laughed (alcohol may have had something to do with it): 'No, we didn't run, we just dived! Look at my scratches!' Since boars can reach speeds of 30mph and plough through the thickest wall of thorns, their efforts would have been futile if the animal had decided to attack. What is certain, however, is that hunters are leaving food out when the female boars are on heat, which means they subsequently have even more babies. 'Now no one can handle the situation,' said my village informer as we sat outside his council house, looking cautiously around us: 'it's up to the government to ban the practice.'

Instead, the hunting season has been extended, despite a third of the population claiming to ramble and only 4 per cent admitting to hunt. Each year, despite a fall in the number of hunters, the season seems to nudge further into the times when walking in the mountains is free from those tinklings of anxiety and their sharp, concomitant explosions.

It has to be said that the men with guns have become friendlier in recent years, rather as most politicians or tax officers have realised that a ready smile gets you further than asocial grumpiness or outright aggression (many bosses, alas, have yet to learn this). *Chasseurs* who don't have behavioural issues have understood that the countryside is a shared territory; we, in turn, read signboards on hiking paths urging us to appreciate that (in my own translation for a local map-making enterprise),

HUNTING IS A LOCAL CUSTOM DURING AUTUMN AND WINTER, LIKE HERDING AND FORESTRY. IT ALSO SERVES TO REGULATE THE NUMBERS OF INVASIVE WILD ANIMAL SPECIES SUCH AS WILD BOAR. IF YOUR VISIT COINCIDES WITH THE HUNTING PERIOD, PLEASE BE RESPECTFUL OF THIS ACTIVITY AND DO NOT HESITATE IF THE OCCASION ARISES TO ASK THE HUNTERS FOR FURTHER INFORMATION ABOUT THEIR HUNTING CUSTOMS.

And, in addition, KEEP YOUR DOGS ON THE LEAD.[1]

Some signs are less official, and show opposition. Recently, high up on Mont Aigoual, I spotted a small metal plaque propped against a beech tree, its message scrawled in yellow paint:

LA CHASSE C'EST POUR LES PDS ET LES BATTUES POUR LES BASTRINGUES [HUNTING IS FOR GAYS AND BEATS FOR NIGHT CLUBS].

[1]On the subject of translation, I am itching to be asked to work on the hunters' own bilingual warning signs. *CHASSE EN COURS* remains the literal CURRENT HUNTING. This is beautifully – rather than painfully – wrong, almost in the same category as the sign I saw in the village square of Roussillon: NO PARKING ALL OVER THE PLACE (*DEFENSE DE STATIONNER SUR TOUTE LA PLACE*). This was topped only by the wonderful DANGER: ZONE OF SINNERS (*DANGER: ZONE DE PÉCHEURS*) in Saintes-Maries-de-la Mer, since removed.

A few months ago, however, I went with the spirit of the times and chatted to a hunter looking anxious on a remote forest path, next to his four-by-four with its back cage wriggling with hounds. He had lost his best dog, while another had been severely injured by a boar's tusks. *Les chiens de chasse* here come in various kinds but the majority are beagles or what we term fox-hounds (hunting foxes is regarded as weird by the French because there is little culinary reward from a scraggy type of vermin). The trained dogs fetch high prices. The hunter's colleague was searching up in the steeply sloped woods. So far that day – it was now mid-afternoon – they had bagged nothing.

We expressed our sympathy a little hollowly and carried on. On our return, approaching the bend where the four-wheel drive had been parked, a gunshot sounded off to our left, unpleasantly close. We began chatting to each other as loudly as we could. It was tending towards dusk, the danger time for unarmed humans near armed members of the species. The same amiable hunter was standing by his vehicle, his colleague a few yards away in among the trees descending into a ravine: he appeared to have been aiming at a bird.

'He's fed up,' said our new acquaintance, 'he's having a go at anything.'

'I hope that doesn't include us,' I joked.

All of a sudden, close enough to make us jump, the gun went off again. Leaves floated down around the man's luridly orange cap. He came back to us looking much more silly than cross. His friend commented that he would, in his present state, have missed a tree if it was one metre in front of him, and then had to remind him to break his rifle. I smelt pastis. A day's supply of victuals, including the generous *arrosage* of the requisite two-hour lunch break, if combined with a disappointing day, encourages last-minute compromises with safety (to put it mildly). It is, after all, a sport of the people, and not just for the nobs as it once was before the nobs were sorted: a touch of the rough-and-ready is all part of the enjoyment.

We were glad, in the folding light, to hurry on away from the duo, who were soon bouncing past us in their four-by-four, giving us a cheery wave.

'The boars live to breathe again,' I said.

'And so do we,' added Jo, with an audible note of relief.

14

Disaster Area

Our flat in the centre of Nîmes is part of a venerable building co-owned by two other people. The *assemblée générale* of the three owners always involves a flaming row, usually about money. Last month's was no exception, and as our gathering takes place on the café terrace at the foot of our building, it is all embarrassingly public. The *syndicat* consists of M. Lafont, the burly locksmith with the stentorian voice, strong Midi accent and conservative views; M. Roger, the owner of a now bankrupt ceramics factory; and myself, timidly proposing this and that while the other two build up to the climactic moment when the locksmith announces his resignation as the 'unpaid' syndic in a dreadful roar that echoes around the square. Just as well we only meet every few years, instead of (as officially required) annually.

The problem is that our four-storey corner building, dating back to the Middle Ages on the oldest street in the city (Roman, of course, but long, narrow and twisting), is not easily divisible into three. What we hold in common is the outside fabric – walls, load-bearing floors and roof. Then it gets complicated. M. Roger owns the ground area, which includes the café opening onto the square and, giving onto the street to the left of our front door, a tiny shop which, until shortly before the meeting, was selling cheap party shoes of the gold and glittery sort. M. Lafont, the locksmith, who despises anyone who is not an artisan (I believe writers fall into the latter category, but I've not yet managed to persuade him), owns the two small flats on the first floor: one is permanently in a state of restoration, full of his tools, its walls knocked frighteningly back to bare stone, while the other is occupied by a succession of tenants. My wife and I have the rest: namely, the second floor and a converted attic.

The roof leaks every time there's a bad rainstorm, its terracotta tiles vulnerable to wind, cats or human trespass; my earlier sorties through the Velux skylight window to find displaced tiles ended when I was caught on one of the steeper areas by a shower, which renders the terracotta as slippery as ice. I groped my way back from the various cliff-edges, where only a gutter lies between you and the pavement far below, but my vertigo now gets the better of me. M. Roger has conceded that he should contribute to a yearly *remaniement* by a properly harnessed builder, even though his own property doesn't get dripped on directly.

More contentious are the cramped entrance and staircase, which lead only to the three flats. A large hook on a bar under the stairs points to the presence of a well underneath, which I have long fancied excavating. The *entrée*'s pitiably dilapidated condition, with crumbling distemper peeling off the soft 'Pont du Gard' blocks of limestone, is primarily due to M. Roger's refusal to contribute to a part of the house that his tenants never use. Not having a cleaner, I sweep and swab to almost no avail.

My stretched sympathy lost some tension last week when he recounted his travails since our last meeting. Apparently, the tenant of the tiny shoe shop, a scowling young man who framed its plate glass with flashing purple bulbs, has done a bunk ('back to Morocco' in M. Roger's words), leaving a smashed-up interior and €9,000 worth of unpaid rent. M. Lafont interrupted my murmurs of sympathy with the claim that he had had to fork out an additional charge for the shop's water, simply to avoid having the supply cut off: €21. The amount sounded pitiful, and M. Roger made the mistake of shrugging it off. Over the locksmith's rising indignation ('It's the principle, the principle, why should I pay your debt?' 'Monsieur, by law I am not responsible for the debts of my tenants!'), the even sadder tale of the café unfolded.

When Henri had taken it over some years back, it became a café-restaurant and the smells grew buttery with hints of charred sirloin. As the pressure of failure mounted, the menus grew starker and the dishes surprisingly low in price. We were living in France, but it smelt like England. Eventually, dismissing our corner as 'a disaster area' ('*une zone sinistrée*'), Henri sold the lease to a threesome of amiable, square-shouldered women, who moved into the tiny flat below ours. They gutted the café, turning it Spanish-sombre apart from a large rainbow in the window: just around the corner, down a narrow alleyway, lies the city's famous nightclub for gay men, so perhaps this was a stab at gender equality. The new sign said 'Casa Chicas', the lettering swiftly defaced by a scrawled 'Las putas'. Free tests for HIV were offered *sur place* along with the tapas, and there was a modest Friday night disco. The furniture was light. For a year or so, everyone was happy. One of my more heavily body-pierced and tattooed art students (she had befriended the three for a while and started the disco project), warned me never to eat there. 'It's filthy, they don't even wash themselves!' I knew there had been a tiff, but I reassured her that I was unlikely to test their *steak frites*. 'Thanks for the tip, though.'

The chief advantage to us was that, because of a dramatic drop in clientele, the noise level sank. All three women were heavy smokers; they kept a tiny dog; the staircase felt even more authentically seedy. I tried pretending I was Hemingway in 1920s Paris. Looking down from my lofty study on the odd tourist innocently tucking into the day's sirloin, I hoped my student's comments were just the result of spite.

The women threw in the towel like their predecessors, the staircase air cleared. We awaited the next lot with trepidation, our proximity to the cathedral and a primary school theoretically ruling out any kind of nightclub: but practice tends to overrule theory. After a brief hiatus, the tables reappeared with paper covers sporting quotes about food from Rabelais, Flaubert and Daudet, while the blackboard offered curried pork or 'spaghetti au fromage', the last resort of those with meagre culinary gifts. According to the new owners, a couple in their forties, the trio had had enough. 'But we'll do things differently,' the woman added crisply from behind the bar of what now called itself a Brasserie.

Expressionistic bullfighting scenes were painted inside and out and everything was served – including beef – on predictably peculiar plates. Despite the daubed toreadors, the refurbished interior was still dark and dingy, the terrace funereally empty under its black parasols. Looking at the three other busy cafés in the square, I decided that our corner was cursed.

The crisply confident couple then also did a bunk, owing €25,000 to poor, long-suffering M. Roger: French law favours tenants over landlords in the spirit, presumably, of the Revolution. Wicked landlords may be a literary trope, but wicked tenants are probably just as common. The café had no takers for six months, much to my relief, but eventually a Moroccan couple arrived, warm-hearted and friendly. Fatima cooked a delicious tagine and served authentic mint teas. Our hopes rose. This was the context in which our syndic meeting took place: among the tables of the café's latest incarnation – bright and tasteful with Arabian curves and pale violet walls. 'I did it all myself,' explained Ajwad, who has what looks like a bullet scar on his forehead and a half-white eyebrow, along with a voice vying with M. Lafont's in decibel level. 'I used *tadelakt*, our traditional chalk paint. You have to apply it in one go and on your own, or the pauses and transitions show up.'

Towards the end of the meeting, M. Roger agreed with me that the café now had a chance to thrive. The business of the €21 surfaced again. I quietly slipped a €20 note under M. Lafont's saucer. 'That makes me even more enraged,' he boomed, shoving it back. The only time he has spoken to me without booming, in 15 years, is when he told me recently that a new tenant had just moved into the small flat on the first floor. The previous one, following the square-shouldered female trio, had sublet to a barman with tattooed flames licking at his jaw, ankles and wrists: a human inferno.

I asked whether the fresh arrival was a man or a woman. He whispered a conspiratorial reply, which I had to get him to repeat twice, hoarser each time, my imagination whirling with possibilities.

'*Il est transgenre! Ni homme, ni femme!*'

He mimed absurdly exaggerated breasts and a short skirt (revealing an unlikely talent for mincing) and said, again *sotto voce*, that he only realised the gender when he saw the identity papers. 'As long as he pays his rent, I don't care,' he added, like someone out of a Zola novel.

His mime turned out to be accurate. In the spirit of officialdom, M. Lafont sticks to 'he' when discussing the new arrival, while I can't use anything but 'she'. Even our building's tenants seem divisible, and just as confusingly so. A little yappy terrier accompanies Claude whenever she goes out, and she likes to spray the staircase with liberal helpings of magnolia air freshener, to which I appear to be as mildly allergic as to the cigarette smoke it overlays.

As she's a native of Brazil, the odd spicy waft rises up the staircase at meal-times, stirring our taste buds. So far, we have not been invited. Oddly clad strangers insistently buzzing our bell, occasionally signalling to me from the pavement with obscene gestures or passing us on the stairs with furtive glances, point to her belonging to the world's oldest profession. Hemingway would have been delighted.

15

Martens in the Roof

Up until last week, the only marten I had ever seen up close was dying. This was over a decade ago. It had crawled into our 'barn' and looked at me with uncharacteristic plaintiveness, even when I came near. Normally, armed with its 38 razor-sharp teeth and badger-like claws, it would have leapt for my face. I left out a saucer of milk and when I came back it was empty. Soon after, I found its long, slim body stretched out in our garden, its beautiful fluffy tail, somewhere between a fox's and a squirrel's, limp as a feather duster. Poisoned, I assumed, probably by something intended for rats. I buried it in our little animal cemetery, along with the cats, goldfish and rabbits who had accompanied us through the years. I identified it, thanks to Google, as a stone or beech marten, close cousin to the pine marten. Few people know much about them, as they are mainly nocturnal.

This spring there were noises in our living-room ceiling. I am a ratophobe, and feared the worst. Our cat brings in brown rats almost as large as herself, depositing them in my study in a mutilated state. Fortunately, I glimpsed a bushy tail disappearing into a gap above the balcony's gutter. 'We have martens,' I told Jo. 'But the upside is, they'll keep the rats away.' The Romans kept martens as deterrents against vermin, in the days when every wild creature was much more numerous. Martens are now a protected species, so there's nothing we could have done, anyway. The downside is that, although sensibly shy of humans, as they mature they get very noisy – chattering and tussling with each other – and very smelly: they eat everything, and do not clear up after a meal. 'They are fond of raves,' as one friend put it.

A litter consists of three or four youngsters, who are nurtured by the mother for three months until forced to fend for themselves in their adolescence. The fathers are always absent. The marten is hyper-sensitive to both sounds and smells that are not self-produced: joss-sticks and mothballs and loud music can be enough to persuade them to up sticks. On the other hand, familiar sounds and smells can reassure them. We glimpsed the mother's tail a few times over several weeks. When we spotted a juvenile wandering about on our balcony, we rejoiced but approached cautiously. It is rare to see martens at all, let alone so close, and we took photos, identifying it as another beech (or stone) marten rather than a pine marten from the way its handsome white chest bib divided into two, running down each leg. It is a beautiful and endearing animal, despite its weasel-like ferociousness when threatened. This one's colour was a deep chestnut. We assumed it had tumbled from the eaves, and wondered how to help it return. It was now nestling almost at ground level in a recess in the wall, big enough to take its slim form. Its youthful, curious, sharp-snouted face was adorable.

Fetching the cat basket, I encouraged it to enter by tapping inside the recess with a pole. It backed in deeper, without making a sound, then emitted a sudden, unearthly screech a hundred times larger than itself with a lunging movement of its head. I leapt back in shock, dropping the pole. Chipmunk-like chatterings over a low growl were interspersed by further screeches and lungings. It struck me, once I'd recovered, that the screech was a kind of missile defence system before the need to retaliate: evolution's gift to a small, no doubt tasty mammal. It was certainly enough to persuade me to put away the basket and construct, out of a ladder, plank, chairs and a table, a climbing frame that reached up to the hole in the eaves. I had read that they were skilled climbers, but maybe not when youngsters. I also put out a shallow bowl of water, as the day was warm and dry. By now it had settled in and appeared to be asleep, sweetly curled, as if sensing that we meant it no harm. We were hopelessly besotted, and it could have got away with almost anything.

Later in the day, after the long sleep, I was astonished to spot it inching up the wall, using its broad claws and pressing its body against the gutter's downpipe in the angle to give it extra leverage. Ever since I spent hours, as a boy in the Congo, entertaining myself through those long tropical days without TV or radio by watching squadrons of red ants on manoeuvres on our bathroom wall – they would even line up to be inspected by the captain's feelers – I have harboured a suspicion that non-human creatures are far brighter than we realise, or dare to realise. They may not solve equations or write books or walk on the moon, but their extraordinary intelligence is of a different order, and is certainly not trashing the planet. This stone marten, young as it was, had worked something out. It had seen the opening and gone for it. Perhaps it hadn't tumbled carelessly onto the balcony. Perhaps it had copied its mother and deliberately descended to explore. It reached the horizontal gutter and hopped onto the roof, from where it lowered itself into the hole in the eaves with one sinuous wriggle.

My theory was proven the following day. We were having breakfast on the balcony when we noticed a slim, furry form sliding from one pot to the next around the edge of the wall. It was in no hurry. Our cat, a keen hunter, watched it nonplussed, without a single twitch of the tail. For Phoebe, this sight was no doubt normal, especially at night. She knew her match. Far stronger and more vicious than a brown rat. Not to be bothered with. A marten recently killed a domestic cat in Germany. Presumably because of the familiarity of our smells, and of our voices heard from birth coming up through the ceiling, the marten did not react at all when we started speaking, or when we shifted to watch it better. It felt secure, it wasn't watching its back. If we had approached too close, it would have screeched and chattered, then leapt at our faces (if sufficiently pushed). There was comfort in its coolness, as if the pure wildness resident in our house was accommodating us. It was a kind of pact. Maybe this was why the Romans preferred them to rats, whose parasitic cunning makes us uncomfortable and disgusted with ourselves. It lapped at the water and began climbing back, flattening itself against the wall as before and inching up with hardly any claw-holds on the limewashed wall, increasingly confident, almost gecko-like. Our cat was already nodding off.

A few days later we saw, lying up in the gutter near the den's opening, a massive thigh bone, no doubt that of a wild boar. The marten, or two of them, must have dragged it there somehow and found it too big for the hole. The next day it was gone. I asked Jo if she'd removed it. No. Somehow, they must have squeezed it in. There didn't seem to have been any meat on it, but maybe the marrow would provide protein, and their jaws and teeth would be exercised. There was an air of enterprise about these creatures.

Over the week there was a sudden increase in noise: thumping, skittering, the same screeches. For periods of 10 minutes or so the rave metaphor served well. We could live with it, if it was not too frequent. And then one late afternoon, Jo saw what looked like a puddle on the sitting-room floor. We looked up. The ceiling was dripping every few seconds, and a circular yellowish patch had appeared. 'Just like that scene in *Tess of the d'Urbervilles*,' I remarked. 'With wee instead of blood.' A faint whiff of the byre.

I bought mothballs the next day. We already had joss-sticks. I lit several and the draught under the eaves sucked the smoke into the roof space. I tossed the mothballs in for good measure. A bit of a fuss overhead the following morning, and Jo swore she could hear the sound of suitcases being dragged, a huffing and puffing, a 'where've you put my socks?' squeal. Within a day or two there was silence, but I tossed in a few more mothballs when we thought we heard a thump. The increasing summer heat baking the roof-tiles may have discouraged them, too: they are fussy about temperature.

Where had they fled to? A month later, I found their loo in the garden. Very like badgers in their toilet habits, they dig a hole first. The scats were unmistakably marten-like, full of colourful berries and seeds. Unless, of course, we had a resident badger, too. But I prefer to think that they didn't want to lose our reassuring scent, and simply moved up the road into their own flat somewhere in the bushes where they can rave as much as they like.

16

A Visit from the City Police

The would-be *tagine* restaurant below our flat has been afflicted with the same curse as the others before it, dwindling to a rather scruffy café with mainly male *habitués*, and offering takeaway pizzas no one buys. The scruffiness is mainly due to each of its large panes of glass displaying spiderweb cracks and what look like the impact of bullets. At least it's quiet. I regret the Moroccan fare, particularly Fatima's apricot-scattered tagine in its earthenware pot, and told Ajwad so. His mistake, he admitted, was to try to drum up business in the neighbouring *quartier* a street or two north of ours. He didn't realise, being an *ingénu*, that this area is miserably poor and popular with heroin addicts (many of them ex-Foreign Legion, whose vast barracks lie off a main road out of town just a mile or so up the hill). Ajwad's enthusiasm is catching, even among the dejected, and within days the results were evident: a clientele of sullen appearance happy to stay half the day on the terrace below my study without consuming more than a cup of coffee. Even tourists don't come near it, congregating in the other cafés in the square, which are thriving.

Sensibly, Ajwad has sublet the business to a young man called Aziz, whose initial zeal has taken the familiar downturn, although a white-jacketed waiter with embroidered cuffs is perhaps a more recent indication of renewed hope. Nevertheless, the stocky form of Ajwad remains a familiar, even ubiquitous sight; not only does he hold forth volubly from his former business premises, mostly into his mobile phone, his apparent fury echoing off the buildings around and putting any lingering tourists off, but he has leased several empty *commerces* on our street and turned them into unquantifiable stores offering internet services, canned drinks, sweets, mobile phones and a medley of dry goods. A much larger space a few doors up is destined, according to the posters in the windows, to become a 24-hour supermarket with fresh fruit and veg, but has been held up in a dispute over the old-fashioned metal security grille which the Nîmes authorities, having entered the UNESCO city bid and intent on removing anything that might clog the works aesthetically or environmentally, wish to see replaced. 'I've told them where to get off,' Ajwad told me – and, as usual, the rest of the street.

With all this commercial gobbling up, along with his vocal decibels and hail-fellow tendency to greet acquaintances, including myself, with a hearty clap across the shoulders followed by a squeeze and a cry of *mon frère* (even if you have already met that day), Ajwad has become the street's godfather with bewildering rapidity. If anything, his black leather jacket, half-white eyebrow and forehead bullet scar helps the impression.

Godfathers attract trouble, however. Quite big trouble, for a few weeks last year. The tiny rentable space just to the right of our front door, not to be outdone by its big brother facing the square, also sprouted a crack on its plate glass – a window, as someone jovially remarked, bigger than the shop itself. Having remained frozen in the vandalised state to which its late keeper had assigned it, the space had been suddenly cleared a few days earlier. 'A pâtisserie,' Ajwad had boomed in answer to my enquiry. 'Moroccan specialities!'

We were delighted, but once the 'gang of yobs' (as he called them) had taken another boot to the newly cleaned panes, his plans were stalled.

Eventually a set of primitive metal shelves was erected, and a small blackboard unfolded in front, with *Alimentation 7 sur 7* scrawled in faint chalk under a Fanta sticker. The promised provisions consisted of no more than fizzy drinks; bottles of lurid *sirop* jostling the odd beer; and truly bumper packets of crisps. A rota of youthful personnel, frequently gathering on the pavement in their fake leathers or drawn-up hoods, with their muzzled, stud-collared dogs tautly held on steel-chain leashes, would make our own exits and entrances a tiresome process. Nevertheless, I initially greeted them chummily on the basis that just because they looked like drug dealers from *The Wire* (a TV series we were watching at the time) didn't necessarily mean that they were. The universal response was a surly glare, as if the use of my own front door was a nuisance to them.

I avoided ticking them off, even when I had to struggle in or out with the shopping or my bulky leather briefcase, dating from the 1960s and reassuringly solid. It was worse for my daughter, home from university. 'They just stare at me,' she moaned, giving a decent impression of a sex-starved zombie.

Our pavement threshold had become, almost overnight, their territory. This is temporary, I kept telling myself. I was particularly nervous of the tall, sporty-looking number in jet-black tracksuit and shades with a silver chain around his neck: he manned the half-empty shop on a full-time basis and either ordered the others around or talked intensely and urgently into his mobile. All my instincts told me that, while the others were possibly playing a role, or had fallen into crime through debt and desperation, he was serious, the type to be working out regularly and admiring his pecs. He had a squat, pug-nosed sidekick – pitted cheeks, face liberally pierced with studs, clad from head to foot in over-large denim – who also worried me. A trainer was suspended by its laces from the permanent wire slung across the street for the yearly Christmas lights: this, I already knew, was a signal to clients that the desired goods were nearby. I wanted to consult with Ajwad, but was told that he and his wife were visiting family in the Maghreb.

Like an unsubtle film, things swiftly hotted up. Mercs with tinted windows cruised very slowly past our door, while more men with nothing to do slouched at intervals further up the road. They might as well have been wearing tee-shirts with JE SUIS UN CHOUF printed on them ('*chouf*' being slang for '*guetteur*', or look-out). I discovered (by asking not them but Google) that your standard look-out made 50 euros a day and risked 10 years in prison. I was starting to get really annoyed, particularly when I learnt how much the tall one in a silver chain was probably earning. On passing the *choufs* on my way to work at the art school, I took to staring at them with a decent citizen's disapproving expression, but stopped when I noticed they would get on their mobiles immediately, the next lot up then watching me with an unhealthy interest. Somehow, the idea of being 'dealt with' in front of my students was even more alarming.

Yasmine, in the chocolaterie directly opposite, was furious rather than scared: it was bad for trade – her customers being mostly genteel, silver-haired women with a penchant for top-quality Belgian chocolates made on the premises. The street being at its narrowest here, the two worlds were but a few yards apart. What she didn't know until I told her was that, at around 10 at night, the little shop's black blinds were drawn down, the door locked from the inside, and some sort of extra business continued on until the early hours – judging by the edging of light around the blinds. I had spotted kids going in, boys aged 12 or 13. Runners, possibly, terrorised into participation. In our very building! What annoyed her most of all was that there was no attempt to hide anything. 'Where do they think this is? The *cité*? Casablanca? Such cheek!' Being Moroccan herself, she didn't have to mince her words.

'I guess we ought to tell the police,' I said, being careful not to glance too suspiciously through her plate glass at the men stationed opposite. I knew for a cast-iron fact that at least two of the local police force's motorcycle fleet were hooked on hashish. I didn't want to end up dangling on a rope as an informer.

She shook her head dismissively. 'You don't think the police know? That lot are being watched already. The cops are just biding their time. They have to know when to swoop.'

'As long as there isn't a shoot-out. You know how it is. Innocent bystanders.'

She handed me a truffle praline with a comforting smile. 'Just be patient. Oh, and here's one for your wife.'

A few days later, at the end of an exhausting ten-hour shift, she flipped. She told me afterwards how she'd locked up shop, turned round and caught them ogling her, and let fly at them. 'I know what you're up to! You're just trying to ruin our *quartier*, to bring it down to your level! You disgust me! You're not wanted here! OK?' Apparently, faced with her tirade, they looked shamefaced. What, even the tall guy in black? 'Well, maybe not him.' I told her to be careful – adding that, if they came for her, she should offer them some distracting *truffes*. Her laugh was heartening.

Jo joined me on a modest reading tour across the Channel. On our return, the tiny shop was closed, the blackboard folded inside. No one hovered on the pavement. The café was its usual desultory self. Yasmine told me that the armed cops had swooped on Thursday afternoon. 'Just like that.' The tall one in black (*I knew it!*) had been bundled into the squad car and was now in prison awaiting trial. 'They've got something on him,' she said. 'Robbery with violence, or worse. They've turned the place upside down.' That would have been hard, I thought, given its meagre furnishings, but it did look a mess.

For a month or so, the odd window-tinted Merc continued to cruise slowly past, and dodgy guys in shades occasionally hovered by our threshold, looking perplexed rather than menacing. Someone – possibly the returned Ajwad, who'd claimed to have had nothing to do with the 'stupid' choice of tenant – stuck a handwritten sign on the shop's glass door: NO PARKING IN FRONT OF THE WINDOW, PLEASE. Since there were no goods to display, and no vehicle could possibly park there without blocking the entire street, this seemed like another mysterious signal. Accosting me a little later, Ajwad offered the space to me (for a nominal price) 'for your car, *frère*. No more parking charges.' He was clearly no longer subletting. The cost was absurdly small, as would the car using it have to have been.

One late afternoon, the front-door bell buzzed. I opened the sitting-room window and looked down. Four men: two positioned at the corners opposite, two looking up at me. One flashed a card. 'Police,' he called up. Plain-clothes, evidently. I hurried down, imagining some family disaster, and opened the door to the card-flasher, short and bald and dressed in a pale blue puffa jacket and brown slacks. His expression was unfriendly.

'We're looking for the gang of young men that live here.' 'Not here,' I replied, chuckling at the very idea. He frowned. 'Who does live here, then?' He was trying to peer in past my shoulder. I was conscious that what he could see – a cramped stairwell whose peeling cream distemper and bare steps hadn't been touched since before the Great War – would have instantly fuelled his suspicions. After all, he was a detective.

'Well, me, with my family, we live here. Monsieur Thorpe. I co-own the building,' I added, reckoning this would make me more authoritative.

He glanced across the street at his own *choufs* in their sunglasses, stationed opposite and on the corner, who now appeared distinctly twitchy. 'And who else?' I stepped outside to indicate the windows above us. 'Well, I live at the top with my family, the flat on the first floor to the left is being done up by Monsieur Lafont, who owns it . . .'

'Empty?'

'Yes,' I chuckled again, a little more nervously, 'but I can assure you that it's uninhabitable, full of tools. And that one to the right is rented out.'

'To whom? This man here?' He was tapping on the male name above the letter-slit in the antique door.

'Yes. Except that he's not . . . Well, he's in fact . . . He's a woman, *pour dire vrai.*'

'*Hein?*'

'I mean, not officially . . . He really is one, though. *Une dame.* But officially, you see, he's still a *monsieur.*' I was floundering under his confused gaze; he didn't even hear the word *transgenre*. Instead of a criminal gang, he had unearthed a mad Englishman busy digging his own judicial grave with every sentence. 'Anyway, she lives on her own. With her small dog.'

I then pointed to my left, to the tiny and empty shop. 'There were a few young people in there,' I said, feebly. He shook his head. He evidently knew all about that lot.

'Or you could try the café,' I suggested, pointing the other way, feeling like the rat-like squealer who gets done in without any audience regret. 'The pizzeria, *en effet*, these days,' I added, as he still looked confused.

'Someone's made a real mistake,' he growled, as if it was my own, and repeated our address. 'They said they were here. Right here,' he added, jabbing a finger past my elbow. Fleetingly, I imagined them secreted in the empty flat, hunched under their hoods, slipping in and out without us having a clue.

He refused to tell me why they were of such interest, just adding that he wanted 'to talk to them', and made no attempt to enter, despite his trio of heavies. Somehow, I must have been convincing. The four men left with a last desultory glance up and down the street. I gave my own ocular sweep of the terrain before stepping back in, turning the lock firmly behind me, twice. I paused on the way up before the empty flat's ancient door, stripped of paint but not varnished. I even listened out for shufflings.

I didn't think I would mention this visit to Ajwad, although I did tell M. Lafont.

Then, almost overnight, the little space became a barber's shop, lined with mirrors and faux-leather chairs, the window filled with large posters of young men in 1970s haircuts. Its open door revealed a shadowy, murmurous interior, with barely room between the knees to swing a pair of scissors. At the time of writing, custom is picking up, but the barber himself, a friendly man in his forties from Meknès (a city we stayed in and liked), still spends much of the time forlornly smoking on the pavement, reminding me of the village wig-maker in *Madame Bovary*, who Emma watches 'walking up and down, from the *mairie* to the church, gloomily awaiting customers' and who longs 'for some shop in a city.' Nîmes is a city, but at times it feels as small and predictable as Emma's Tostes. He informs me that Ajwad has just left for Morocco 'definitively'. He had too loud a voice – an observation which may well be metaphoric as much as literal. '*Un charlatan*,' he adds, with no need now to keep his own voice down. 'He owes money to everyone.'

I indicate my overgrown, chestnut tangle, admitting that it's mostly been cut by my wife for the last few years, and book an appointment for the afternoon. I anticipate further revelations in the barber's chair. He looks pleased. 'By the time I've finished,' he says, chuckling, 'there won't be a trace of your wife left up there.'

17

Arches and Bulls

The urban practice of *flânerie*, perfected in the nineteenth century by the likes of Flaubert and Victor Hugo ('*Errer est humain, flâner est parisien*') demands effort and will: strolling idly about with the senses on alert is too easily put off for busier pursuits, not least squinting at your mobile phone. The area of Nîmes north and east of our apartment, outside the historic centre, is perfect for the true *flâneur*. The inhabitants range through all the classes bar the upper, most streets are not yet done up and the many eighteenth- and nineteenth-century buildings, from grand to extremely modest, are tinted in the sooty brown coat of long neglect. This is even true of the grand house or *hôtel* built by the renowned antiquarian and botanist Jean-François Séguier, a neglected *érudit* whose library and collection of fossils ('*empreintes*', as they were called at the time) made Nîmes even more of a compulsory stop on the European Grand Tour.

The crumbling façade stands almost within view of the Porte d'Auguste, a main Roman gate that straddled the Via Domitia: a route long before the classical period, it linked the Alps with the Pyrenees, running right across southern Gaul. Hercules and Hannibal used it, one in legend and one in fact. The gate was originally embedded in the city walls, which took four miles to embrace the city. Originally flanked by a couple of forbidding towers, it has archways for wagons and smaller ones for pedestrians, the sills well worn in each case by wheels and feet. A couple of carvings of bulls are faintly decipherable above, along with an inscription citing Augustus as the donor; this priceless 'document' was mostly destroyed – like much else of historic interest – in a fit of misplaced enthusiasm during the Revolution. Fragments of the ramparts turn up in cellars and behind shop walls. The surviving flagstones of the road passing through the arches remind me of Pompeii's alleys. It's an enriching place to pass by almost daily.

Every city is a palimpsest, but in Nîmes it is flagrant. One of the largest cities in Roman Gaul, its population was an estimated 25,000, descending dramatically to 1,000 – scarcely double that of our village – by the fourteenth century, the result of plague, economic collapse and serial occupation by Vandals, Visigoths and the Umayyad Caliphate. Yet it swiftly recovered and much has survived, especially underfoot. Major works in the square opposite the gate turned up the burial ground of a medieval monastery. For a month or so I could look down on the latest skeleton staring bemusedly up at the unmonkish twenty-first century, the bones flinching at the sharp buzzing of scooters. At one point there were several in view, like a ghoulish dormitory. I still see them under the fancy new fountain and trendy benches.

The late conversion of a long Haussmann boulevard into a Ramblas-like pedestrian thoroughfare lined with trees and jetting fountains revealed, not the anticipated artisanal workshops on the edge of town, but a huge, wealthy villa torched so abruptly that non-inflammable items like mosaics and metalware were left intact. Learning of one exceptional mosaic currently being exposed and soon to be transferred to a laboratory, we hurried down to the railed-off site and entered with the striding confidence of experts. We stood for at least two minutes before the great oblong of tesserae, its featured god hazily basking in the sunlight after a couple of thousand years under charred beams, soil and tarmac, before a member of Inrap (Institut National de Recherches Archéologiques Préventives) shouted at us. What most struck me was how unused we are to seeing archaeological items before they are restored and cleaned: the mosaic was a muddy monochrome of sepia, like an old photograph.

The discovery nearby of three tombs went unreported: each contained a male skeleton, their heads turned the same way. Towards Mecca, it is now established after several years of meticulous research: these bones are the earliest trace in France of a Muslim presence, dating from the eighth century – the time of the Arab expansion in North Africa. They are thought to be Berbers integrated into the army of the secular Umayyad Caliphate that ruled the city for several decades with the collaboration of its inhabitants (on retaking Nîmes in 737, a vengeful Charles Martel, history-book hero of the Front National, typically reduced much of it to rubble).

Even minor works reveal something. Next door to the flat, on the neighbour's hammered-at façade, a relief of St George spearing the dragon appeared through the scaffolding and dust. Tools were downed until the experts had been. The lovely medieval carving remains in place, suitably restored. A refit of the public garden behind the nearby city museum, lowering the level by several metres, sprouted an intact and slender Roman column. Pale in the moonlight, the ground in shadow, it was like a message shot from the gods. A few days later it was gone, as phantoms must be.

Not every layer is classical. At times, on my way to the underground car park, I picture a little boy playing hopscotch beneath the arches of the Augustan gate. We are back in the 1840s, and the boy's name is Alphonse Daudet. Nîmes's most famous literary offspring was the author of, among many other books, *Lettres de Mon Moulin*, brilliantly witty provincial stories intended for a Paris audience.

There is an upper room dedicated to him next door, in the old-fashioned family bookshop and *papeterie*, the famous Lacour-Ollé, started on the back of a pedlar's cart in 1791. The 'museum' is a kind of shrine with soft music, storyboard panels and the odd memento: Daudet's promiscuous ways and eventual syphilis are somewhat skated over, as is his anti-Semitism. He was born around the corner in 1840; the rather grand boulevard house was left for a smaller one in the suburbs when he was seven. His father, a silk manufacturer, had fallen on hard times. Daudet's increasingly impoverished childhood was said to be unhappy, although the surrounding streets and parks compensated somewhat in the days when children could roam freely. He described Nîmes as having, like any Midi town, 'a great deal of sun, quite a lot of dust, a Carmelite convent and two or three Roman monuments'. One can sense, perhaps, the slight sneer of a provincial become a metropolitan sophisticate, although he never quite lost his local accent, 'like a faint hint of garlic' according to a friend.

To add to the time-warp sensation, much of the shop gives onto a nineteenth-century covered arcade, le Passage Guérin, built some 30 years after Daudet's birth and an intact example of the once-fashionable forerunner of modern shopping centres (a long-vanished Parisian equivalent provided the memorably gloomy setting for Zola's *Thérèse Raquin*). Ollé's display includes the publisher-bookshop's own numerous titles as well as life-size suits of armour, rows of plastic skulls in gaudy colours, faintly erotic bronzes, brooding figures of a hooded Death, marble busts of Louis XIV, ancient Egyptian replicas in black and gold, and lethal-looking Japanese swords. Familiarity has blinded me to the sheer oddity of it all, rich with suggestion, more Balzac or Flaubert than Zola. Passage Guérin also includes a barber's, a Portuguese delicatessen, a key cutter, a dentist's surgery behind heavy oak doors, and an organic café-restaurant where there was once a useful haberdashery.

A slingshot away is the Maison Carrée, a small pillared temple that is the best preserved anywhere thanks to the antiquarian efforts of Séguier; anywhere in this case being the old Empire, stretching from the heat-shimmered Red Sea to a rain-lashed Hadrian's Wall. Henry James thought it 'exquisite', while Thomas Jefferson was overwhelmed, perhaps encouraged by the sheer steepness of the approach steps – whose sole embellishment is, rather disarmingly, my own acronymic initials carved deeply into a riser near the top: A N T.

Jefferson found the temple to be 'the most perfect and precious remain of antiquity in existence. Its superiority over any thing at Rome, in Greece, at Balbec or Palmyra is allowed on all hands.' He promptly had it copied for the Virginia State Capitol building, where it triggered a fashion for pillared façades throughout America.

Until recently, the interior boasted a 3D film recounting the city's history: when the spears jabbed, I rather embarrassingly ducked. Recently restored and then cleaned by laser, the temple has a glowing ivory perfection, reflected in the glass walls of the ultra-modern *médiatheque*, or library-cum-arts centre, that faces it, designed by Norman Foster. The huge transparent volume brilliantly embraces not only the bright sunlight that so struck the architect on his first speculative visit, but a centennial *micocoulier* (hackberry) that might otherwise have been in the way. This contemporary masterpiece goes some way to offsetting my Spenglerian thoughts of cultural decline at every sight of the beautifully proportioned temple – in which you worshipped Augustus, of course, Rome's very first emperor and a living deity.

Nemausus was, in fact, where every Roman official hoped to be posted: blessed by sun, nestling on a vine-growing plain scattered with luxurious villas, peaceful inside its stone girdle of walls, with a state-of-the-art amphitheatre and limitless water brought across 31 miles of dry, rocky terrain by a sinuous aqueduct. Faced with a serious obstacle to the latter's completion – the volatile River Gardon in its gorge, prone to flash flooding – the Romans built what still remains one of the world's greatest *ouvrages d'art* (as 'engineering works' are so beguilingly called in French). While I'm no great fan of humanity's tendency to defy the physically impossible – gargantuan proofs of our own self-worth, projections of existential insecurity while Nature cowers – this particular multi-arched example, the Pont du Gard, takes the breath away. It is built in the same soft stone, *pierre des Vers*, as our flat – the large creamy blocks visible on the upper, distemper-stripped section of our staircase.

Like all such human feats, there is something absurd about the Pont du Gard. Water carried over water! It is so high that, in the days when tourists were allowed to walk along the top (as I did when on a childhood trip), with no guard rails before the cliff-like edge, they were regularly blown overboard by the gusts funnelling down the river valley. Or so locals claim. 'You can see the individual memorials scratched into the stone,'

I was told by a trustworthy Nîmois. 'Crosses marking the spot, and so on. Most of them were Dutch,' he added, with a wink. 'It's because the Dutch are so tall. You know? Like trees in a gale.'

The structure that impresses me most of all, however, is the aqueduct itself, of which the Pont is a mere brief section, like the celebrity star of a production involving thousands no one remembers. Unshowily, keeping to an average gradient of 24.8 centimetres each kilometre, falling to an undetectable 7 millimetres per 100 metres at some points (achieved without the use of laser measuring by God knows what technique), frequently passing through dripping tunnels, the stone serpent brought its 400 litres per second on gravity alone: the endpoint, a round limestone water tank with lead pipes distributing the water over the city, still survives up a long and narrow street near the university. A very rare example of a *castellum divisorum*, yet few tourists bother with it.

Like my garden watering system, the working aqueduct found its chief challenge in limescale, along with local landowners illegally tapping the water to irrigate their own nearby fields. Nevertheless, it lasted five centuries until the final apocalypse of the barbarians. The whole thing is a metaphor for writing a novel, of course: you complete the impossible *ouvrage d'art* and the waters flow, to be delighted in or defiled, until it reaches its demise on the shelves of a charity bookshop, its conduit having been punctured by self-proclaimed reviewers on the internet or apathetic judges of literary prizes.

Incredibly, this gargantuan, millimetrically precise structure was a top-up: loving their fountains, ponds and elaborate baths (their daily consumption of water was higher than our own, per capita), the Roman citizenry had outdone the gallons still bubbling up from the ever-generous spring in the present and immensely attractive Jardin de la Fontaine, France's first public park. Nemausus was the native tribal goddess presiding over this liquid abundance, the water drawn from the hills and mountains as far away as our own slopes in the Cévennes: the Roman method was usually to conquer and absorb rather than conquer and destroy (as long as you agreed to adore the Emperor), so they not only named the city after a local goddess but also made a sacred precinct of her spring. Swans glide over the gurgling, glittering surface of the *source*: this is a spot I am drawn to when inspiration weakens. It helps that Henry James, embarked on his own consciously provincial ramble (*A Little Tour in France*, 1884), once leaned on this very same parapet and gazed into the basin 'full of dark, cool recesses, where the slabs of the Roman foundation gleam through the clear green water' and thereby experienced a memorable epiphany: 'it seemed to me that I touched for a moment the ancient world'.

He was not so keen, however, on the pre-Roman tower at the top that all paths lead up to over the slopes of steep Mont Cavalier: he wrongly identified it as medieval, calling it a 'dateless tube'. The Romans sheathed it in stone cladding, much of which has come away to reveal the Gallic original. It was probably a look-out or a signalling station in a visual chain: you can see for miles from its top. Its pale stones catch every nuance of light, but my attempts to paint it in oils were more successful in catching polite comments from passers-by than the thing itself.

The liquid generosity of Nemausus still provides, and new Europe-funded fountains gush, but such natural abundance has never been enough, at least not for the progressive, restless element of *Homo sapiens*. In this respect, the topping-up aqueduct and its attendant bridge can also seem a metaphor for human foolishness, that hollow lust for prestige. Sustainability is not glamorous. Common sense never is. Who in their right mind would have invented plastic without considering its afterlife?

'Stupidity,' I had initially written, before scotching the sentiment as too extreme. I had entirely forgotten that the word was already used by James himself when describing both the Pont du Gard and the amphitheatre. Both bore 'a touch of that same stupidity', but of the oval arena in particular he added, 'It is brutal, it is monotonous, it is not at all exquisite.' Yet he also found it – or at least the fact that so much had survived – 'wondrous'. I share his ambivalence, especially given that the arena's sand is still soaked by the blood of beasts, poked and punctured to resounding cheers.

You can see *les arènes* from our third-floor roof: a creamy-white streak in the terracotta sea, this being 'the rim of the monstrous cup – a cup that had been filled with horrors', as James put it. Some years ago, I took Jo's cousin, a university professor of classical sculpture, to a bullfight in the afternoon. Knowing he was a practising Buddhist, I was a little nervous. The spectators clapped and roared. As the fierce sun glared from limestone blocks and fawn-coloured sand, glittered off the clinging suits of the toreros, picadors and banderilleros, turning each bull's punctured back into a sheen of red satin, he leaned towards me with a delighted look on his face and said, 'This is the closest I've ever felt to the Roman world!'

The colossal arena was probably started during the Flavian dynasty around AD 70 and is the best preserved in existence. Its cliff-like bulk is a troubling presence in the relatively small historic centre, and not just because of its violent associations. It looks solid, despite a certain surface flakiness, but it isn't. The drystone blocks are splitting and there is serious seepage. Several years into a massive restoration project, and the finished segment gleams like tiered icing, casting the remainder into an even grubbier state.

One of the arches is topped by another sculpture of bulls, equally disfigured by two millennia of weather but a reminder of the longevity of our enthusiasms. Modern bullfighting came to southern France from Spain some 150 years ago (it is banned elsewhere in the country). Otherwise, the arena's perfect acoustics serve bands like Radiohead or singers like Björk, the volume much higher than is required and spilling over the surrounding rooftops like boiling milk in a pan. Around the rim, with no safety rails, individuals sit dangling their legs over the giddy, 70-foot drop or gyrate perilously to the beat. I recall the corrida that, because of a cancellation the previous day, was packed with twice the numbers it should have been, helped by the presence of the celebrated torero El Juli. I spotted my then-fifteen-year-old son sitting on the edge of a massive block of limestone in a non-seating area between the tiers, the equivalent of three storeys of air separating him from the bullfight's little figures below. This was far more suspenseful for me than the *tercio de muerte*.

The Romans were at ease with their cruelty, but for modern Westerners it is hidden away, or glimpsed on a screen, or processed into abattoirs and chicken factories. Watching a bullfight does remind me, however, of what beasts we are: it takes a matter of minutes to turn a peaceable if bewildered grass-chewing creature into a tortured cadaver dragged around with chains. The smaller, more agile local bulls are reserved for the bloodless *course libre*, the huge black Spanish bulls for the killing game. Reared happily out of sight of humans in the wilds of the Camargue, they are pepped up and weakened a few days beforehand by various unpleasant methods: when it comes to the fifteen-minute finale, these rippling slabs of muscle have no idea what to make of the small, lanky figures darting about the ring, as these awaken no echo in their brains. What one does feel is their extreme disappointment not to have broken out of darkness into their familiar sunlit pasture.

Strange, then, that in the complex iconography of the corrida, the bull is symbolic of death.

Whenever I visit *les arènes*, usually in blazing heat, it is the cool breath of the *vomitoria* (exit passages), smelling of the underground galleries where machinery and victims were stored long ago, that brings that momentary Jamesian 'touch' of the ancient world. The chill draught seems full of the fear once felt by gladiators and animals alike, phantasmally crouched in the gloom beside doomed followers of an obscure prophet called Jesus. The hidden galleries – like giant corridors – once communicated with the exterior: lions, leopards and other exotic species could appear like magic, with a primeval force similar to the modern surge of the black bull through the wooden gate and into the light, bearing whiffs of straw and dung.

The corrida is technically illegal under European law, which bans the torture of animals, but an exception has been made for the 11 *départements* where it is regarded as traditional. For many years, I meekly went along with this local culture, persuading myself that a bullfight is the last echo of pagan ritual; of lost Minoan practices; of Theseus facing the Minotaur; of Mithraism and prehistoric battles with aurochs – of which the Spanish bull is only too visibly a direct descendant. It helped that Hemingway was a regular visitor, always booking the same room in the Hôtel Imperator, while Picasso preferred the Cheval Blanc opposite the arena. Both believed that bullfighting was not a sport but an art, like ballet, and sufficiently interwoven with Catholic iconography to bring it a glint of the sacred. Along with Cocteau, Coco Chanel, Jean Dubuffet and others, Picasso would watch and cheer from the shaded front row of the bottom tier, as close to the action as possible. I occasionally experienced a kind of transcendence when the bull and the matador were in perfect harmony through the silence of some 16,000 people collectively holding their breath, the bull transfigured into a gambolling feline. But the last corrida I attended was some seven years ago. The bull was close to me and seemed to explode in crimson at the so-called Moment of Truth. I left early in disgust.

Even keen aficionados like my friend M. Barnier, a retired letterpress printer who once produced poetry pamphlets for my one-man publishing house, agrees that disgust is a legitimate reaction. For three generations, in a street adjoining ours, his family printed the city's bullfighting magazine on an enormous Heidelberg Platen, which continued to wheeze and clatter until a few years ago, and which now resides in the stockrooms of the Musée des Cultures Taurines, a poem by the Irish poet Vona Groarke (from the last of my pamphlets that M. Barnier produced) frozen in lead in its frame. He and I often cross paths in a café in the pretty Place aux Herbes, and discuss the joys of feeling the print like faint braille on the paper and the shoddy nature of so many recent books. His main complaint about bullfighting, however, is that the Camargue bulls have weak knees unable to support their vast tonnage when the going gets rough. 'It makes it safer for the torero,' he says, with contempt, sipping at his espresso.

The pros and cons of the corrida is a subject to be avoided in this city, if you wish not to fall out with those you have always regarded as friends. It is, I suppose, a kind of code of silence. Nevertheless, anti-corrida demonstrations are becoming more frequent. The latest, outside the amphitheatre itself, featured the *Baywatch* actress Pamela Anderson draping herself for a few minutes in front of the life-size bronze statue of the legendary Nimeño II, which was subsequently sprayed by 'an orange liquid'. The presence of a Hollywood star ('just there to show her *cul*,' commented one aficionado) ensured a febrile international media attention. Nimeño was tetraplegic after being tossed by a bull in 1989, and subsequently hanged himself in his garage in an outlying village 'like a washed-up farmer', as *L'Observateur* put it. I did once see the superbly brave Sébastien Castella, whom I first watched when he was a teenager, have his thigh snagged on a horn. This is potentially lethal, but the horn missed the crucial artery.

For the past few years, the arena has hosted historical re-enactments of Roman games, including chariot races and gladiatorial combats, with a cast of hundreds: these have included the battle of Actium, in homage to Augustus, the city's chief benefactor. This in itself is accurate: the Romans would flood the arena for their re-creation of famous sea battles, the gallons piped directly from the *castellum divisorum*. Maybe this was all the excuse they needed to spend five laborious years and a fortune on the aqueduct. The brainchild of Eric Teyssier of Nîmes University, *les Grands jeux romains* might, in the bold if realistic view of the *Midi Libre*, eventually replace the city's twice-yearly bullfighting feria, during which the arena's sand is thumped by the bodies of some 50 bulls and the streets run with booze. Like many living in the centre of town, we escape to the hills. The idea of a replacement is appealing, although the absence of real blood and unabashed cruelty makes these re-enactments, at heart, very un-Roman; I doubt Jo's cousin would be terribly interested, for all their painstaking accuracy. Bar the odd forgotten watch or pair of glasses among the leather-skirted soldiery, you are looking at something theoretically indistinguishable from the real thing.

Among the many books about Nîmes printed by Lacour-Ollé, there are lots on bullfighting, including *Daudet et la tauromachie*. The author was an enthusiastic spectator, but the book includes his eyewitness account of a young *banderillo* – a handsome local – being eviscerated against the barrier on a single agonised scream, 'still holding the two *banderilles*, which quivered for a moment like a signal of distress'.

A few days ago I went into the shop for pens, paper and salvatory paperclips, squeezing past the fading maps and curled postcards in their outdoor stands. A tabby cat similar to our own, curled over the unfaded *OLLÉ* fired into the nineteenth-century glazed floor-tiles, got up to brush against my legs. It had turned up a month ago and wouldn't leave. The antique fan, suspended from one of the blue-painted ceiling roses, revolved slowly in the summer heat. I asked one of the staff for the cat's name.

'Alphon—' she began, instantly correcting herself with a laugh: 'Auguste, I mean.'

Between Caesar Augustus and Alphonse Daudet, the city's shadows still flit and waver. Meanwhile, for the last month or so of summer swelter, Auguste has appeared on a Missing poster, a spectral presence looking out at passers-by in the arcade's half-light with what is, one hopes, a merely teasing air. When I asked about him last week, old Madame Ollé, now in her nineties and still serving customers, told me a story of the war. She and her family were bombed out by the Americans ('they never much cared about what they hit') and again by the English ('they were much more precise'). They moved four kilometres away, from near the marshalling yards to the safer side of Nîmes, taking their cat with them. Then he disappeared for a month. 'That's how long it took him to find his way back to the bombed-out house,' she said. 'My mother took food every day, since he didn't want to leave, even though it was a ruin. I think that's what has happened to Auguste. He's upped and gone back home, wherever that is. Home is so important, *n'est-ce pas?*'

Wherever that is. And that's the mystery. I nod a touch too enthusiastically.

18

Defending Wolves

The worst thing about the wolves, say the shepherds, is that you don't see them. They prey on your mind, because you can be certain that they're out there somewhere. Perhaps behind that juniper bush. That oak. A whole pack, maybe, beyond that low tussocky hill where you'd take a bite to eat in the old, wolf-free days. You know it for sure when the dog, usually afraid of nothing, dedicated to defending the flock, is suddenly shivering against your legs. Refusing to go a step further. Ancestral memory, this, because no shepherd around here has faced the wolf menace for six generations. Never mind that some 150 generations of local pastoralists had to live with it before; it's now been forgotten. Finding the disembowelled lamb and its mother, stragglers both, fleece torn, insides spewed out, is a deep psychological shock. It's personal, the shepherds say – those of them who can express their emotions freely. Others just bottle it all up, then have a nervous breakdown a year or two later. This is what the doctors report.

Like many people, I am fascinated by shepherds. Many years ago, before the wolves were anywhere near our mountains, I remember meeting a wizened *berger* tending his flock in a steeply sloped chestnut wood, the air November-damp. The sheep were munching eagerly on the chestnuts, muzzling them free of their spiky armour, their neck-bells translating their excitement. 'It keeps their fleece oily, protects them against the cold and wet,' he said, leaning on his knobbled stick, watching as they ate. During the war, and other hard times, whole communities were kept from starving by chestnuts, just as they have been for many millennia in China. The 'bread tree', as it was known here from the sixteenth century, grew well in granitic areas where olives and cereals were not suited to the acid soil or the altitude, and whole forests were planted. There is not much you can't do with chestnuts, from soup to black bread to roasted kernels, and they are stuffed with fatty acids and nutritional goodness. Locals, too poor for much else, gorged on them.

Thus the dismay when, in the 1960s, the canker *Cryphonectria parasitica* decimated their numbers as seriously as the 'ink disease' of the 1890s. Careful arboreal treatment and a fashion for chestnut purée saved the industry. We gather them in season, careful only to stick to those tumbled onto the paths. There is a childlike satisfaction in heeling open the hull, spiked like a medieval flail, and revealing the glossy fruits nestling inside like cubs. Now a different kind of natural threat is endangering shepherding itself: if one of the main reasons for the Cévennes mountains' recent designation as a UNESCO World Heritage Site was the Neolithic survival of traditional 'agro-silvo-pastoralism', then so also was their diversity of species, including the wolf. Like the vulture that feeds on the kills, *Canis lupus* is protected. Hunters are forbidden to shoot it. Officially.

The shepherds (like the goat herders) know all their animals by name. Even when the flock numbers five or six hundred. Their quirks, their characteristics, their personalities. The outgoing ones, the insular ones. The leaders, the followers. Through the long and lonely days outside, the continual presence that Mediterranean pastoralism demands, you learn respect and fondness. So when just one of these familiars is hideously torn apart and left (not necessarily eaten), your view of the world, of life, changes. The world becomes less kind, more threatening. The ewes miscarry in the ripples of fear, and paranoia sets in. That's what the Cévenol shepherds say, and some give up.

The defenders of the wolves – from expert specialists to straightforward Greens – say we understand, we sympathise, but *tant pis*. The wolves were here long before us, long before language, long before the concept of agro-pastoralism (defined by mobility and transhumance), or the human race or even the furry-looking hominids with the beetling brow and long-limbed crouch. This is their rightful territory, their heritage. We can't appropriate it completely, as we have appropriated so much of the planet.

Flocks of sheep, some of the defenders remind us, are destructive to wild flowers, to saplings, they leave a hillside ecologically stripped. Along the gennel behind our house there are so many wild violets in the spring that their scent fills the air. Years ago, an old lady from the nearby farm came to pick a bouquet. 'When I was a child,' she said, 'these were all eaten by the sheep. They loved the violet taste. We had to get up first thing before the flock passed, if we wanted any for the house.'

Do children still pick violets? Or even know what they are?

Well, wolves at least have returned, spreading back up, not from Poland as was previously believed, but from the Abruzzi mountains in Italy. We must learn to live alongside them, their sympathisers say, now that they have decided to hang about here on their passage to the Pyrenees, an epic journey built on cunning and intelligence. Since the red deer was reintroduced, it is worth it: serious meals are readily available.

It's too easy for later immigrants like ourselves to find the natives troublesome. Look at what happened in the United States. In Arizona, lying under the brilliant stars in an Apache reservation 40 years ago, I suddenly sensed this vast brashness of a nation as absurd, outrageously appropriating the tribal lands for what is, let's face it, a gain so short-term that it can barely be called a way of life. More a way of death, perhaps, and on a planetary scale.

When we walk in the mountains, we sense the wolves these days, as we sensed them in north-eastern Romania, up in the Pagan Snow Cap Region where the shepherds have dogs fiercer and more dangerous to walkers than the wolves themselves. Even these dogs are helpless against a whole pack. We sensed the bears there, too. There are no bears now in the Cévennes.

Our friend Max lives with his family high up in the neighbouring commune, having spent years single-handedly restoring a *mas* burnt out during the war by Waffen-SS troops from Nîmes. Yurts now dot its fields, and the self-composting toilet stands proud, with an amazing view down the plunge of valley. The first evidence of wolves was a dead badger on the three-mile forester's track up to the house: 'Its stomach was ripped open but only the liver was taken, being the most nutritious.' Then, returning home one day in his jeep, looking across the wooded gulf, he saw a large animal padding past the front of the *mas*. 'Too big to be a dog. And the hairs were standing up on the back of my neck. Even at that distance.' I nodded: they say that looking into the eyes of a wolf changes you. A few weeks later, up on the nearby col, his own dog abruptly cowered, refusing to move a step further, and it now hates going up there. Soon after, on the very same windswept crest, a neighbouring shepherd's fearless border collie began whining and trembling . . . and there was the wolf itself, slipping between sprays of wild broom. The park officials arrived the next day, armed not with guns but thermal imaging cameras.

'Personally, I am happy,' said Max. 'My dream is to wake in the middle of the night and hear their howls. But I'm not a shepherd.'

Rumour has become fact. They have returned. They have arrived *chez nous*.

Perhaps that's what the locals thought when they saw the Waffen-SS soldiers tumbling out of their armoured cars, fanning over the same hills, intent on rooting out what the officers reckoned was a thousands-strong army of Resistance fighters. There were no more than a few hundred, of course. One of the victims was young Fernand, only son of peasant farmers, not a member of the *Maquis*, who had been ordered to guide the troops to a remote hideout of the Resistance. When they arrived, there was no one: only a few beds of bracken, the embers cold in the hearth. They torched the house and shot Fernand through the back of the head halfway along the return path, out of spite. It took days before he was identified (laid out in the *mairie*) by his clothes, as his face had gone. We always pause by his memorial plaque, and Max keeps it alive with flowers.

There is no real comparison between the self-conscious savagery of those soldiers and the sleek beast they modelled themselves on, its violence powered by instinct, but the Nazi regime made it all too frequently. 'I am the wolf and this is my den,' Hitler commented to a servant in his mountain hideout, and as early as 1928, Goebbels described the Nazi delegates to the Reichstag as 'like a wolf tearing into a flock of sheep, that is how we come!'

In our early years here, a hike in the remoter, higher parts was likely to take us close to the wolves, watching unseen; now the same might be said of a local walk. The chill you feel is in response to the purely feral, and to the canniness of a creature who has learnt to cope where we have only learnt to conquer. It adds grit to the comforting blandness of the term *Parc national.* The wolf doesn't obey boundaries. Its limits are those of its own survival. That's why it avoids us, stays concealed, ready to put distance between it and the threat – at least 60 miles in a single day if needs be. Ancestral knowledge of how dangerous we are, shared with so many in the animal kingdom, is what keeps it alive generation after generation; for instance, the nature of the operation to eradicate it from America a hundred years ago seems psychopathic in its needless cruelty. At some almost cellular level, these things are remembered. As for the danger to humans from the wolf itself, in normal circumstances there is none. Only the shepherd has reason to fear: not for his life, but for his way of life.

The demands of UNESCO-protected pastoralism versus natural wildness, or shepherds v. wolves, were enacted in the form of a mock trial up at Florac in the high Cévennes recently, with real barristers, witnesses and a judge hearing the evidence, the whole procedure streamed onto the Net and taken very seriously.

The wolf knows nothing of such shenanigans. *Canis lupus* came before, and it will continue long after all our human quarrels, all our greatest concerns, have abated into birdsong and wind.

19

A Catastrophe

It is Friday morning in the hills. A clear-skied late June. We have barely slept, but we have to shop, and fancy a river swim. On the track where our car is parked, we meet our occasional neighbour from Normandy. He has recently retired as environment inspector, no longer ticking off EU stipulations. He drove down yesterday to his second home, escaping the rain. '*Vous allez bien?*' he asks, as if today is normal. We pull appropriately long faces and he nods vigorously. '*Une catastrophe!* It's not the fault of the people, it's all too complex to grasp and they're manipulated. Referendums are a bad idea. God knows what would happen if we were to hold one in France.'

The clear, rocky river is exquisitely chill under the overarching leaves, and we are alone. I enter the water slowly, scattering minnows and a lazy trout. It's like walking into a liquid freezer unit. After a few minutes, however, your body adjusts and you might as well be in a lukewarm bath. Perhaps this is what the post-Brexit era will feel like after the shock: we are good at adapting.

Lying on the bank, I sense my late father shaking his head in disbelief. The Derbyshire son of the village

schoolteacher, he volunteered to fight the Nazis at the age
of 16. The horrors he witnessed in Normandy, Belgium
and Germany made him a committed Europhile. Fluent
in French from his years as a serviceman, he escaped
Britain's post-war grimness by joining Pan Am and
being sent abroad: thus my birthplace (Paris). I once
asked him what the happiest moment of his life was.
'The day Brussels was liberated. Music and dancing
in every street.' The river chuckles on and I try to be
philosophical: the natural state of human existence,
perhaps, is migration. Or war. Without the Union,
Europe would return to its old habits. Perhaps that's
what the likes of Farage, Davis and Johnson want;
belligerence, where the crasser sort of rhetoric finds
a home and bombast rules. I think of Victor Hugo's
celebrated lines:

> Depuis six mille ans la guerre
> Plait aux peuples querelleurs,
> Et Dieu perd son temps à faire
> Les étoiles et les fleurs.

> For six thousand years, war
> Has pleased a quarrelsome people
> And God wastes his time making
> Stars and flowers.

All my life I've tried to put down roots, and failed.

We return to find friends' emails and text
messages: those in French are sympathetic, as after a

bereavement; those in English are distraught. 'My whole life has been mocked', reads one. To questions about what difficulties this might mean for the Thorpes, resident in France for 25 years, I reply 'none at all', as we have dual nationality. Never has that decision, requiring four years of patience and paperwork, seemed more sensible.

A phone call from our friend Delphine. She switched on the radio and thought she'd misheard. She invites us over for a solidarity supper with her husband Yves in the *Hameau* – a cluster of ecological houses deep in the woods, self-built over some eight years without a centime of subsidy. Pierre and Marie appear on the new wooden *terrasse*. 'Ah,' cries Pierre – something of a joker, except when he's driving the school bus – 'you two immigrants still in the country, then?' We sit round salads and wine as the encircling trees darken against an emerald dusk. 'The thing is,' Pierre insists, 'they've pissed us off, slowed Europe down, but we don't want them to leave.' I'm glad he isn't saying *vous*; in the village, we are still 'les Anglais'.

The real worry is that the same will happen in France. Pierre waves his fork around. 'The French seem ever so nice, all happy with their little suburban house and garden, but when things explode . . .' He draws a finger across his neck. A guillotine? 'The Front National first, then real violence. Take Vichy: 85 per cent of the French were *collabos* in the war!' I protest at the figure, and insist that the circumstances were different. Yves reports on the meeting about the anticipated Syrian families to whom the municipal council has offered a big youth centre as refuge, in true Cévenol tradition. 'One bloke who shall be nameless stood up and all he said was, "I'm frightened", then sat down again. A young woman who'd worked in the Calais camp tried to explain and was told to "go back to your own place, you don't understand us here".' She lives 10 minutes away, in the nearby market town.

We all agree that a lot of people are *cons*, especially the hunters. Yves yells sardonically to the forest at large, 'I adore hunting!' and we listen to the echoes with amused dread. I ask if anyone was talking about Brexit in the village café today. Pierre, who often serves behind the bar, gives a dismissive snort. 'Nobody. Not even football. Alcohol! *C'est tout.*' He did, however, discuss the issue with the village's lone Luxembourgeois, who thought the English were 'arrogant' and we were well shot of them. Well, I say, raising my glass, 'at least he's not French. *Aux Français!*' The rest of supper is taken up with an account of failed attempts to shoot a huge rogue boar that destroyed the hen coop, having omnivorously munched through its residents. Maybe Yves wasn't being sardonic, after all. As we bump away along the track, our headlights reveal a large and shaggy hulk with a glittering eye, crouched in the foliage. 'That's him,' I remark. 'Boris himself.'

I'm about to go up to bed around midnight when the phone rings. It's Jacques from down the lane. He's *bourré* and sounds almost tearful. 'I've read what you wrote about Brexit on Facebook. I wish to salute your effort before you depart.' I reassure him that we're not going to be expelled, as we're French. He sounds surprised. In all the 20 years we've known each other, it's simply never come up. '*Je t'embrasse, mon ami. Très fort.*' I picture us hugging each other, like Lear and Gloucester, in a howling storm.

On Saturday morning, I walk down to the village for bread. The economic turmoil I have been hearing about on the radio gives me hope that the decision will have to be abandoned and the dry bank of regret held onto before the whole country is swept away. It would be missed by the French, at least: my students at the art school love our islands' relaxed, informal vibes. Several of them, with my encouragement, have gone over on extended Erasmus sojourns, returning with better English and a stronger appreciation of their own country's food. All this is at risk.

Locals and incomers standing outside their houses slow my progress with questions and commiserations. Carlos, whose parents (like many others in the village) were refugees from the Spanish Civil War, agrees with the others that the EU is far from perfect. 'Can you believe it? They're even fudging the bee issue.' Since the village is trying to turn itself into a non-pesticide zone, this is a hot subject. Under pressure from the ghastly Bayer and, it has to be said, the reliably non-green UK, the Union's banning of the pesticides responsible for the collapse of bee colonies is only for two years, and not total. 'It's the corporations that really run Europe,' we conclude.[1]

The modest Saturday market feels emptier without the bulk of Laurent, booming jokes from his big white butcher's van ('Would you like a bit of my thigh with that?'). He's away in Ireland for the salmon fishing, his chief passion. Lisa, our painter-*boulangère*, greets me with a look of concern. 'The thing is,' she says immediately, reaching for a warm baguette, 'it's the old versus the young. Only the young should have voted. After all, it's their future that's been cocked up. The old will be dead and gone.'

She's interrupted by Rémy, the former mayor, standing behind me, who has burst uncharacteristically into song. A grumpy, *ultra-gauche* detester of all incomers (he 'lost' our naturalisation papers for a year), racked by arthritis from working his organic smallholding, he seems peculiarly merry. I have to admit that he has a fine voice.

---

[1] In November 2017, the UK government finally agreed to a total ban on neonicotinoids in the face of the alarming evidence.

20

Floodwaters

U ntil the October rains, the heat had been unremitting since late June. The relief arrived with the abruptness of a slammed shutter, and the cobbled path behind our house became a torrent. Two ancient stone uprights, knee-high and with a single vertical groove in each, stand either side of the back door: they puzzled me until a local told me they were to block the floods with the help of a board slotted in. It works well. Without that defence, the water rushes enthusiastically over the sill and spreads through the room, for when the rains do come, it's always with a kind of bottled-up, monsoon zeal: the equivalent of Paris's annual rainfall can fall in a single day. The temperature drops abruptly, fresh breezes waft through. It is pleasant, if disconcerting.

The mountains and steep valleys of the Cévennes produce micro-weather patterns, so that one village can be soaked while its neighbour stays dry. The area's proximity to the sea, separated from the coast by a large plain, creates a unique phenomenon known throughout the world as *l'épisode cévenol*: warm air from the Mediterranean strikes the mountains and swirls into the autumnal currents of colder air arriving from the north: the result is an unstable spawning ground for tempest and flood, anticipated to worsen with climate change. On 3 October 1988, the equivalent of the Seine poured through the centre of Nîmes for seven hours, drowning nine of its citizens. A grand piano was filmed floating down the street, and has become an abiding image of the trauma, due mostly to human idiocy: ancient retention basins (known locally as *cadereaux*) had been built over. Hundreds of millions of euros have been spent replacing them.

A few years later, our village found itself in the eye of an *épisode*. Neighbours gaped at water rushing through their living rooms, especially where ancient discharge tunnels had again been stopped up thanks to modern ignorance. In the old houses built on the hillside, the rather off-putting staircases, steep and straight, were turned into cataracts, although these proved harmless once you opened the front door. 'Never try to stop water having its own way,' as old Albert explained years ago. 'Wave it through. The quicker out, the better.' Parked cars from a less appropriately adaptable era were unceremoniously swept off and the streets gouged out, displaying the recently installed sewage system. We all knew the builders had done a botch job, back-filling with rubble, and here was the proof. The village was declared a disaster zone, but patched itself up in a few weeks.

This was nothing compared to 2002, however. After a friend's wedding, we set off *en famille* towards our newly acquired weekday flat in Nîmes. We knew there might be rain, and the wind was oddly warm and moist. Suddenly, the daylight deepened to twilight and buckets of water were hurled at the windscreen amid raw-boned cracks of thunder. The robust main road, originally Roman, was replaced in minutes by a river sliding across with mud-brown equanimity. We watched a foolish car approach tentatively, reach the middle and stop. The driver tried to get out as the vehicle began to be nudged sideways. Cars are fine in floods until they become boats, as a volunteer fireman once put it to me.

'We'll try the back way,' I announced, the storm still in its juvenile phase, but no sooner had we hit the twisting country lanes than it had fully matured, our windscreen wipers smothered by liquid lashings as loud as hurled pebbles. The false twilight was deepening to a premature midnight relieved only by flashes of bolt lightning. The floodwaters, pouring down the vineyards and olive groves, had turned the steep verge on the left into an endless weir that spilled across the gulley of the road, the level rising alarmingly fast. As we crept forward, I feared our old Renault station-wagon was beginning to lose its grip, and our narrow shelter would become our doom.

We reached a small village on a hill and stayed put, to sit out the evening and much of the night in an empty, unlit street. I quoted King Lear, to my family's dismay: 'Rumble thy bellyful! Spit, fire! Spout, rain! Now please go away!' Like our Nîmes flat and our village house, the car leaked: water gathered in the footwell, the odd drip struck our necks. But we were alive – and hungry. I loped to the door of the house opposite. I was ushered in by an old lady paddling in rubber slippers through several inches of water that lapped at stolid oak furniture. 'Oh,' she said, as I expressed alarm, 'I've got used to this, over the years. I was born here and we've always survived!' She was much more concerned about the three children, and gave me a packet of Petit Beurre and a bottle of Evian. Such resilience was heartening: the storm had been boxed safely into historical precedence, and what seemed wildly beyond control was tamed and contained.

Back in the car, as we munched our biscuits, we were blinded by a flash, its sharp explosion bouncing the vehicle: a lightning bolt had struck just yards away, instantly followed by its sinister aural companion. My children wondered what would happen if lightning hit the car itself. 'You stay calm,' I advised, heart still racing, 'then take a jump. Don't touch the car and the ground simultaneously.' Over the storm's two days, the Gard *département* would be struck 60,000 times.

A fire engine stopped behind us and a fireman emerged. He shouted that we were not to stay in the car, it was too dangerous. We could sleep in the village hall. Under bright neon, around a hundred people and accompanying blankets were failing to nod off in plastic bucket chairs or on the floor. Orange juice and biscuits were being distributed. We decided it was not for us, and during a lull made a break for it, inching past a landslide's spilled boulders and reaching the roundabout on the main road. I asked some firemen next to their vehicle whether it was safe to carry on, given that the rain had eased. 'As long as you go right now and take care!' They seemed peculiarly agitated: a call had come through. Another body had been recovered. The fifteenth, one of them shouted.

The gleaming black camber stretched towards Nîmes, occasionally under shallow sheets of water like molten metal, but we reached harbour – the lightless city centre – without incident. When the storms resumed a few hours later, and the rivers delivered their full load, it ripped up the main road like liquorice. When it was all over, 80 per cent of our *département* had been underwater at one time or another, and 24 people were drowned. It could so easily have been 29, I reflected.

Rain is good, as the locals put it, as long as it doesn't arrive all at once. By early September, most years, with the spectre of wildfires haunting the parched vegetation, you are willing on the first rumble of thunder. Climate change means we should expect even more extremes, but this autumn's downpour was all bluster, merely bringing out the buckets (terracotta roof-tiles can only take so much water at a time). The hills have been plumped into greenness again, their southern scents unbottled. This is no guarantee that the next episode won't be a more direful spectacle. As Lear implies, storms return you to the origins by addressing all the senses with one elemental message: there are no messages. This is how life began, and not necessarily for any reason. Not that this philosophical attitude helps when it comes to it: in the eye of a storm you feel the entire world convulsed and crumpling, and all your old realities are so much broken rigging.

21

The Ballot

The 2017 Presidential election was the climax of an extraordinary year in French politics. It began with a prospect about as enticing as an Arctic ice sheet: either the Catholic right-winger François Fillon or the extreme-right Marine Le Pen; the Socialists were disintegrating in the wake of catastrophic approval ratings for the outgoing President, François Hollande. Then their centrist Economics Minister, Emmanuel Macron, announced he was forming a new party. The ice began to thaw, but the result was cracks and confusion. The over-confident Fillon became embroiled in a corruption scandal. Macron was sweeping up support with his youthful fervour and sheer charisma. His main rival was now the far-left Jean-Luc Mélenchon. The stable two-party system of old, left and right, with the *Front National* an ominously growing third force, was disappearing. Which floe to join? Which would carry us to safety?

With the ballot for the first round of the Presidential elections already underway, I was still an *indécis*. So was a quarter of the electorate. The evening before the vote, dinner with a large group of friends had resolved nothing. All French (four of North African origin), they had grown impassioned, shouting simultaneously and waving their hands. Everyone present was more or less divided between the two main candidates. One or two regretted (as did I) the fate of Benoît Hamon of the socialist party, who was backed by the Greens. He had already fallen to 7 per cent in the polls. A vote for him would be wasted. I observed that Macron was a fan of that most *engagé* of writers, Émile Zola, so he couldn't be that right-wing. Our old nightmare – a second round between Marine Le Pen, whose makeover from fascist thuggery to alt-right respectability was fooling a lot of those impoverished by France's economic difficulties, and the disgraced François Fillon, with links to the ultra-conservative Catholic network, was still possible. How could we vote for Fillon if he made it to the second round, even as the only bulwark against the *Front National*? The suspense by Saturday night was sleep-destroying.

Every French citizen receives a brown envelope in the days before the first round of the election, stuffed with relevant party tracts and small slips of paper, each of the latter bearing a candidate's name in block capitals. One of these can serve as your ballot. I usually slip my choice into a back pocket before walking down to the village. It pays, in a small community, to be secretive about your politics. My wife had reluctantly decided she would vote Mélenchon, but I was still hesitant, despite his ecological credentials: he was too Euro-sceptic. Viper's bugloss flowered on the steep cobbled path, as dependable as ever. We passed clusters of locals outside the café, looking self-conscious. A couple of them I knew to be FN supporters, but we greeted one another with neighbourly bonhomie. Our village is predominantly left-wing, with a hippy underlay, and the atmosphere was surprisingly tense under the morning sunlight.

Or maybe I was being over-sensitive. Although (like Jo) I have dual nationality, and was born in Paris, I am *un Anglais* – a foreigner. The shadows behind Marine Le Pen are dark and dense, populated by SS-admiring tycoons and youthful strategic advisors with iced-over blue eyes. As we approached the *mairie*, our friend Pierre, a fervent supporter of Mélenchon, raised his hand like a gendarme and cried, 'Sorry, you're English, forbidden to vote!' I made light of it. If Le Pen were to win, dark jokes might come true. We entered the old building under its squat clock tower. The two booths looked oddly imposing in the narrow room beyond, where the mayor presided over the slot in the Perspex ballot box. Macron? Hamon? Mélenchon? Their final syllables kicked up in a row like the skirts of a can-can chorus. Never Fillon, anyway!

The queue shuffled forward. My back pocket was empty. I had omitted to bring the ballot. No matter: the official procedure, after registering your presence and receiving a little envelope, is to pick at least two names from the lined-up piles on the table. In this instance, closely flanked by Pierre and others demonstratively choosing Mélenchon, I followed the herd.

Once behind the flimsy, thigh-length curtains of the isolation booth, I noticed a single ballot left on the shelf. Benoît HAMON. Uncreased, almost virginal. I ignored it, folded my paper, placed it in the envelope, closed the flap (no glue, no licking) and re-emerged. There is something faintly absurd about this whole business, I thought, as the mayor flicked the lever to open the slot, the envelope joined the pile, and the cry went up: 'Monsieur Adam Thorpe . . . *a voté*!' Your gesture is infinitesimal by itself, it only makes sense as part of a group, accumulating weight as it moves from village to district to nation. It's an abstract idea with a concrete outcome, able to smash as much as to build.

Outside, we met 95-year-old Ferdinand, a long-retired Protestant pastor and amateur painter whose effulgent watercolours continue to grace the village's annual art show. In contrast with around half of the nation's youth, he had bothered to exert his democratic rights, tottering down with the help of a zimmer frame. He had cast his first vote during the time of Vichy – a regime which Marine Le Pen claimed, just a month ago, '*n'était pas la France*', in a troubling echo of her father's denial of the Holocaust.

The results, at 8 p.m. on Sunday evening, brought relief as well as disappointment. The village had been heavily for Mélenchon, predictably, but he hadn't made the second round. During the fortnight's *entr'acte*, my journalist son arrived to tour the area for the BBC's World Service, visiting boarded-up towns and villages where economic despair and racial tensions provide a feeding ground for the extreme right. Our Gard *département* is one of France's poorest, crippled by factory relocations and agricultural decline, resentful of Paris and globalisation. He found few willing to support Macron openly, and felt unnerved in Beaucaire, whose soft-voiced FN mayor crouched nervously in the town hall like a baron in his besieged fortress.

I helped out by doing the English voice-over for a man interviewed in a nearby market. 'I'll vote for the National Front,' I heard myself saying. 'I find it insulting to be labelled a populist, just because I want more protection.' One can sympathise with the last point, but this was less than a day after the live television debate between the two candidates, whose cacophonic invective was dismaying. As a floundering Le Pen scrabbled for her notes and hammed up the villainess role with a desperate relish, Lady Macbeth came to mind. My dreams were haunted by that grin, disconcertingly like a Francis Bacon mouth. It was troubling to think that an estimated 35 per cent of the French were backing her as President. (Over the ensuing months, we learnt that the dramatic drop in her support was a direct result of that performance, during which Macron mostly kept his nerve.)

Our occasional Norman neighbour with the space-age swimming pool appeared on the eve of the final round. 'Oh,' I said, without thinking, 'aren't you voting?' He snorted. 'What's the point? I voted Mélenchon, and Macron's promotional clip shows a tractor spraying a prairie field with pesticide. He's sure to get in, anyway.' I had also been horrified by the clip, but wasn't his confidence of the same misplaced sort as had doomed Lionel Jospin back in 2002, allowing Marine's father to slip past? For the sake of good relations, I avoided mentioning either this or the pool, which had (as previously mentioned) banished our nearest nightingales.

At least Pierre and family were now voting Macron instead of abstaining. It was lunchtime. We had done our democratic duty and were happily settled outside the bustling café. 'We always end up voting *against* someone, rather than *for*,' Pierre moaned from behind his sunglasses. He was pessimistic: since a majority of the young were plumping for 'Marine' (she had dropped the surname), the future looked grim. 'Brexit, Trump, Putin, Erdogan,' came the litany from another grey-stubbled villager, sucking on his roll-up. 'And your Theresa May,' he added, leaning forward in his chair, '*elle est pire que Thatcher!* She'd have preferred Le Pen to win, right?' I picked up my glass of Pelforth. 'Don't get me started,' I said.

We attended the count in the *mairie*. This involved the mayor reading out either a candidate's name or '*blanc*' (for 'blank') off the unfolded ballots in a stentorian voice that carried to the back of the room, where some 50 of us were gathered, with two council members recording the vote by hand. A tiny outlying hamlet was, as usual, late in delivering the ballots. 'The donkey's lame,' someone joked. Their arrival earned an ironic round of applause. Eventually the total was totted up on a whiteboard. A quarter of the village had voted for the extreme right.

We moved into the café for the final announcement on television at 8 p.m. In the days before I took on teaching to supplement my freelance income, I would visit the bar twice a week. It was worth it just for the jokes, the banter, the old stories. In those days, the *patronne*, Lydie, knew everything that was going on as well as everything that had gone on for the last century: a sepia photograph on the wall, dating from 1902, showed the café with precisely the same glazed doors and, it seemed, the same net curtains, with a group of locals from the past's other planet, including a little girl in a frock – Lydie's mother. When Lydie succumbed to Alzheimer's, her nephew took over and installed a flat-screen television and a tasteful colour scheme that replaced the sombre nicotine brown of yore. She was now sitting at her usual table and greeted me with the fervour of someone suffering short-term memory loss. The café and the *mairie* directly opposite used to be at loggerheads: Lydie's husband was the mayor until he was ousted some 15 years ago by the new guard in a slightly underhand *coup d'état*. If anyone from the Conseil Municipal came in, Lydie would refuse to serve them. This was probably against the law, but no one wished to test it. The two buildings would glower at each other with only the *mairie*'s grandiose perron and the corner of the square between them. These days the old quarrels have abated, yet the room felt tense under the calm, it being election night. Still, no one was refused or told to leave, whatever their views.

When the countdown's final seconds began to flash on the television, most remained on the square outside, apparently uninterested: an eclectic mix of veteran locals and less familiar back-to-earthers under dreadlocks or in baggy cardigans. When Macron's score was revealed as being higher than expected, my wife and I whooped with relief. Foolishly, perhaps; most in the little bar or at the tables outside just turned and carried on chatting, keeping their politics to themselves.

'Welcome to the neo-liberal world!' announced a woman in a long woven dress.

'*On verra*,' said Pierre, '*on verra.*'

22

Paws, Fingers and Thighs

When we first arrived in the village, we had Georges, an amateur archaeologist, and Michelle, his retired art-teacher wife, as next-door neighbours. He had been a paediatrician. When he died, his study — a dusty necropolis of skulls, bones and ancient bric-a-brac from his countless digs — had to be cleared. Michelle had removed most of the more precious objects, and wondered if I would be interested in making an initial foray into the layers that remained. I tried not to sound too vulturine.

Harbouring the illusion that everyone must be equally keen to heap up the litter of the past, I started the next morning. The study occupied a solid stone lean-to with a slit window (ventilation in its hay-storage days) looking out on the back path. I would often wonder what Georges was doing. He did invite me in a few times, and would show me his array of prehistoric skulls, mostly small because they'd belonged to children. I assumed this was to do with his days as a paediatrician, but he dismissed the suggestion. 'Children tended to fall like flies before modern medicine,' he pointed out. The skull he was most proud of, however, was from an adult: charred black, but only on the left side. It had come from an underground cave a few valleys away. The sacred relic, he suggested, of a revered ancestor, set in a niche long ago and lit by a single rush-light, the soot accumulating over centuries. It was a ghoulish object, faintly Dalí-esque, or like a Mexican sugar skull, and I worried that he had disturbed something profound.

Now, some years later in his study, I was about to disturb the silt of his own life. The cramped room's muddle concealed great purpose, intense fascination. All that had separated us from this glorified reliquary was the stone wall of an unrestored part of our own house, where the dim rafters are favoured by bats. I felt a prickle down my spine: this wasn't the disturbance of a single life, but countless full lives of which these stubs of objects and bones were all that remained.

Georges's brain had once been sharp, but over the years it had gradually turned to sponge, cell by cell. Much of the study's contents remained unlabelled, although he had evidently garnered a lot from Cerveteri in Italy, whose famous Necropoli della Banditaccia is an Etruscan site of over a thousand tombs. He had brought these vestiges back to the Cévennes in order to study them at his leisure. Was this legal? Did I have the right to do what I was doing? Michelle had insisted that most of it would be thrown away, otherwise. Dusty drawers in old cabinets revealed beads, lead weights, sherds of glass and pottery, and flat wodges of Roman roof-tile. It was a hoarder's cornucopia.

As I covered the few yards up the path and traipsed in and out of our back door with my plunder, Jo groaned from the sitting-room. 'The house is already a museum, Adam!' I reassured her that this lot was the very last. I went back to thank Michelle. She presented me with a weighty cloth sack powdered with dust: inside were large pieces of an urn. 'Or I'll chuck it,' she insisted.

I heaved it over my shoulder and, like a cartoon burglar, glided soundlessly back through our kitchen (open via an arch to the sitting-room), on my way downstairs to the study and safety. Without raising her head, Jo said, 'I thought the last lot was definitely it.' I mumbled something reassuring and, before I was out of shot, she looked up.

'It's just an urn,' I reassured her, the sack's contents digging into my back.

And what an urn. I stuck it back together like a museum conservator, feeling I had missed my *métier*. A lovely, smooth vessel with a slender foot, about three feet tall, emerged from the ugly fragments. Visible inside were traces of a black substance, like dripped tar. I assumed this was something like decomposed olive oil, that the urn had been ranged with hundreds of others like any modern bulk container. Years later, I was told by a Roman expert that the vessel was a funerary urn. 'That down there is incinerated cadaver,' he said, shining a torch inside. Given Georges's repeated visits to Cerveteri, this made sense.

I look at it now with a touch of reverence and an inevitable question. Who did the cinders, rendered from bubbling fat and bone, fingernails and eyeballs, chitterlings and blood, belong to? A man, woman or child with as much emotional complexity and will to live as myself, obviously. It remains a perfect *memento mori* beneath the long, south-facing window. Not quite a half-charred skull, but close.

Nous tous, les vivants: rien que fantômes, ombres sans poids.[1]

The plunder included chunky fragments of antique rooves. Ancient Greek and Roman roofing was similar to ours in present-day southern France, consisting of interlocking terracotta tiles. The flat type was called a *tegula*, a thick and tapering cuboid with a raised rim on each of the longer sides to channel the rain downwards; they were laid to overlap the tile below, and to sit flush with their neighbours. The inevitable gap between was protected by a curved, semi-cylindrical tile called an *imbrex*. As in modern times, until machines took over, these were moulded on a man's thigh.

One of the recuperated fragments of flat roof-tile, the largest, was twice the size of my hand and surprisingly weighty. It had a label on it, already brown with age, the words paled but in Georges's neat hand. '*Tegula. Empreinte de chien, 2° S*'. (Roof-tile. Dog's paw-print. 2nd century.) And there it was: the trace of a dog that

[1]'All of us, the living: nothing more than phantoms, weightless shadows' (Sophocles). One of the 59 maxims painted on the beams of Michel de Montaigne's tower library.

had wandered into the tilemaker's yard almost two thousand years ago. Two slightly overlapping paw-marks showed, with each of the four toe-pads like a large oval petal. The still-wet tiles would have been taken out of their wooden moulds and spread to dry in the sun, row after row; the animal had padded over them. Cool clay against a dusty tread, the most unmemorable of moments preserved. Roughly one in every hundred ancient tiles or bricks is thus imprinted: the trespassing menagerie includes not just dogs but cats, chickens, pigs, horses, geese – even weasels, martens and stoats. With the occasional bare human foot or hob-nailed boot. Edward Thomas once admired a paw-print in such a tile; yet the England described by the poet in *The South Country*, with its jingling pony-traps, flinty roads, countless larks, sparrows and peewits, its horses nodding before the plough, its total absence of plastic, now feels as far off and foreign as anything Roman.

The more I've studied the *tegula*'s surface over the years, the more I've noticed: tiny coils of ejecta, smudges and scratches and smears, pin-prick holes. I feel like the Mars Rover trundling over the rugged basalt surface of the desiccated planet: its colour is identical to the tile's, and there is even a gulley or canyon a few inches from the latter's top edge, showing squashed clots of clay on its slopes. After some experimenting, I found that my fingertips hooked into this damage perfectly; I could lift the tile vertically by the depressed grip, my palm balancing the weight on the other side. Someone had picked up the tile when it was still soft, perhaps the same person whose fingerprint was faintly visible near the paw trace.

This seems odd: wouldn't the aim have been to produce a near-flawless object? On the other hand, we are looking at something produced on an industrial scale, like bricks. Few ancient tiles have recorded the gouge of a grip. What story lies here? A jobsworth tilemaker picking up the paw-damaged product, deciding it was satisfactory, ignoring his own crude mark?

Most excitingly, perhaps, there were perfect renditions, as if finely carved, of leaves, spikelets and seeds on the rougher side. The tile would have lain in the yard for several days, reaching the required hardness of leather before being fired in the oven's fierce blast. Too much moisture remaining, and a tile cracks or shatters as the traces of water reach boiling point. The yard's grassiness had been pressed into the soft clay through the tile's weight alone. The double paw-print itself included the pressure points of claws, miniature impact craters with rims or flaps of ejected clay on one side. These proved – according to Sabine, our local vet – that the animal was not a large feline (a jaguar, say) but a dog, as cats keep their claws retracted if on the move, even when jumping.

Musing on this tile, I saw tousled life, its captured hazard of a second baked into permanence. As I gazed in turn on the urn, I saw death's smooth and elegant hands, cupping the soul for eternity.

I realised the paw-prints were a natural mould, like those vacancies in the hardened ash of Pompeii left by rotted corpses, where pain and a dreadful end were filled by Fiorelli's plaster into eerie and moving casts. I could resurrect the two paws – one front, one rear – of a vanished dog. They had landed almost on the same spot a fraction of a second apart and thus overlapped in Venn diagram fashion. My friend Bill, actor, poet and fellow ex-pat who owns dogs and horses in the next village, read the prints like a detective. 'He or she is loping along beside the boundary wall, and leaps over several rows of the tiles on the right. A soft landing across the last two tiles in the outermost rows.' He traces the impression with his finger. 'Front right paw flattened for landing, claws high, hind right paw following lightly into almost the same place. And then our friendly cur steps out to the right, pushing off using the left hind paw and so comes onto clear ground. Disappears quietly into the night. Not a sound. There is nothing about these imprints that suggests haste or panic.'

I nodded appreciatively. 'Bill, you should be writing novels. But how do you know that he – or she – pushed off to the right?' He smiled. 'A dog always pushes off with the opposite hind leg. This rear impression would have driven deeper if there was a turn towards the left.'

In humans, the big toe drives deep because so much of our weight is pressing down on it at the start of the opposite leg's swing. Specialists call this the 'toe-off'. It is visible in the first recorded hominid footprints made nearly four million years ago in newly fallen volcanic ash at Laetoli in modern Tanzania, and proves that bipedalism occurred before brain expansion. Three gorilla-like individuals strolled casually along like modern humans, unbothered by the soft, wet ash. Were they panicked by the local eruption? Apparently not. The tracks show no sense of hurry. We receive from them an extraordinarily important signal from our slow and mostly lightless evolution.

Soon after, Bill sent me a photo of the trail of prints left by his 35-kilo Beauceron bitch on wet cement. Weirdly, it was just a single line, the muscular dog tiptoeing over the unfamiliar surface – 'mincing across', as Bill put it – like a human on a tightrope. It had reminded him of my Roman tile, with those two paws keeping in the same narrow track.

So we know how this far-off moment galvanised an animal, bunched its muscles, fired its brain, traced its intention. And with an animal, Bill added, intention is all. And now I'm tracing that moment myself in words. I feel close to the dog, so close I can touch its bristly flank, sense it nuzzling my hand with a cool nose, smell the hot and slightly foetid stink of poor drains on the air, of open effluent in a sluggish river, of sweaty clothes and oiled skin and the evaporating moistness of clay. Of char and wood smoke. A smell like present-day India, only this was the Roman Empire nearly two thousand years ago.

I wasn't prepared for the surprise that awaited me when my friend Stephen recently visited for the weekend.

A sculptor, he's in charge of moulding and casting in Toulouse art school: the kind of expert I needed. We had briefly discussed the paw-print project and he had promised to bring the necessary equipment. There was a knock on the front door. I opened it with a grateful smile, but Stephen was looking down at the old terracotta tiles of our small entrance hall, the former kitchen: square *tommettes* in every shade of red, brown, orange, salmon-pink. The hall tiles are sloped towards the door, to ease rinsing in the days before proper drainage: the dirty water would have been flushed out onto the flight of stone steps and ended up harmlessly in the gennel below. Perhaps this slight tilt helped him to see it: at any rate, he had immediately spotted something in the second row of terracotta tiles near the threshold.

'Ah,' he said, 'there it is.'

He was looking down at what I had always taken to be ordinary damage: several soot-dark, shallow indentations in one of the tiles, which are thought to date from the seventeenth or eighteenth century.

I saw it immediately.

That familiar disposition of pads, front and rear overlapping.

'A big dog,' Stephen commented, as I stammered my astonishment. He was already crouched and taking a photograph, rucksack still on his back.

It was as if the same loping hound had leapt the centuries – some 15 of them, in this case – to vanish out of the front door.

Stephen was impressed by the Roman roof-tile, and set to work the next day. His experiment with a special type of moulding material, which would show up every detail, was abandoned when a test sample in one corner stained the absorbent terracotta. He was mortified, but a brisk rubbing with flour all but concealed it. He hadn't brought any fine plaster with him, but Jo suggested pasta dough, which she duly prepared. It seemed suitably Italianate. Being made from organic brown flour, the lump of dough chimed perfectly with the terracotta shades.

Stephen kneaded it into the double paw-print with his palm. Would the latter be deep enough, I wondered, to produce anything more than a shallow bas relief? We went for a walk in the spring sunlight.

An hour later, the pasta had hardened sufficiently to be able to peel it away. Amazingly, the crisp depressions had become perfect canine pads, oval and the size of hefty grapes, the toes of the rear paw impatiently overlapping the front paw's left toe. The larger back pad on each foot, previously visible as a smudge, were now shallow swellings. This is normal: a dog walks on its toes, it's the four foremost digital pads that absorb the shock of landing, that press the deepest.

I nestled the pasta mould in my palm as an owner might nestle a real paw – one of the most sensitive parts of the animal, complete with scent glands, so that dogs can smell through their feet.

'Fidus Romanus was in good condition,' observed Stephen. 'Quite big, probably young.'

'How can you tell?'

'Here, look – the pads are smooth, no visible wear or punishment.' Not being a dog-owner like Stephen, I am ignorant of such things, of how those incredibly tough, leathery cushions can indicate health problems or become infected from the constant impact of the ground. I wondered how you could have a four-legged creature that leaves only a two-legged trace. 'The grass or the tile next door took the other two legs,' Stephen said, agreeing with an observation Bill had made: that a dog intending to stop on landing might splay its limbs up to a foot apart. Our hound was in no hurry, remember, as it pushed off gently to the right. Maybe someone shouted, threw a stone, but it made little difference. Present-day dogs that trespass in our garden, big lolloping things that dig up new plantings, go for the fish in our little pond, are often surprisingly slow to react to my yell, to the odd warning pebble. Or maybe it all happened after sunset, in the pre-electric gloom, the flicker of the night-guard's fire safely distant and only a pair of glowing eyes giving the intruder away.

From the similar impression in the roseate tile by our front door, its indentations darkened by soot, a much more recent dog must have turned in the same fashion in a French tile-yard some 15 or 16 centuries later. Yet our ghostly, domestic resident feels so much further off: apart from the illusion the Roman period always gives us of a greater familiarity, a curious modernity, the more recent traces are fainter, dimmer, worn by footfall. A kind of reverse echo.

I showed Stephen the other and more mysterious impression: that deep gouge on one side, near the top, like a Mars canyon complete with landslides. He didn't seem convinced until I used it to pick up the tile, my fingers comfortably nestling in the corrugated gash. This is what sculptors in bronze call a 'negative impression'; the hand is the 'positive form', as were the paws. Again, we had to reproduce that positive, and what more basic form than a hand? He now found it intriguing, and reckoned the hand must have been small, perhaps a child's. The pasta this time was a yellowish-brown – accidentally flesh-tinted. My hand pressed the dough into the trace of another hand that had pressed in turn (less consciously perhaps) into the wet clay some eighty generations ago.

Neither of us expected much. An hour later and we were looking at slender fingers emerging from primordial mud. The little finger was a perfect cast, the others more expressionist; a bundle of wriggling worms, as oddly slender as the fingers in a painting by van Dyck. They were the 'inscape' of a hand more than its realistic depiction, with each phalanx bonily clear, as was the stretched smoothness of flesh between knuckles, rendered stronger by the buff-coloured dough of the medium. Presumably the original impression was blurred by movement, by the effort of seizing and lifting. There was certainly nothing static about it. Stephen still reckoned it was a child's hand. A boy slave, perhaps. Or a jejune assistant facing a lifetime of tile-making, its smells and textures and effort already a part of his tired body, mind numbed by the unchanging routine, stirred only by the odd intrusion of an animal. A kind of hypnotic pleasure in the task, all the same. Dreaming of girls, perhaps, the unimaginable landscape of their bodies under the flimsy tunics.

The immense frustration, to me, of not knowing who this hand belonged to. That I was holding it over the millennia without looking into anyone's eyes.

This emergence was as rough-cast and eerily precise as Michelangelo's *Prisoners*, the struggling torsos extricating themselves from unworked marble. Or it was a hand carved by Matisse, so like the fingers that clutch the side of the head in his *Reclining Nude* of 1907 – itself originally fashioned in clay and transformed to bronze through the complicated 'lost wax' process involving multiple moulds. But this hand – or the part of it we could see, the three phalanges of four fingers – wasn't art; it was an actual part of someone's limb. It was the very grip itself, at the same time as it was a reaching up or out, a human gesture rising towards us out of the nameless swirl . . . like something octopoid cleared by an ocean wave and momentarily glimpsed before subsiding back. Back into its own time, into formlessness and oblivion.

I love the fact that the Latin for 'moulding' or 'shaping' or 'contriving' is *fingere*. The physical act remembered in the definition. *Fingere* is the root of the word 'feigning'. And, of course, of the word 'fiction'. Novels are written on the fingers, whether clasping a pen or dancing on a keyboard (in my case, a duo for two digits only). And their prints are unique.

In fact, the marks of long-gone fingers are preserved all over the house (as they are in Nîmes). You have to get up on the roof to see them. The older curved tiles show several shallow ruts scoring the crescent face from top to bottom: this is the drawing up of the fingertips, pressing and moulding the wet slab of clay to the thigh. You can also see a brushing or smoothing over with the palm or loose knuckles, as subtle as wind-trace in sand. On one tile, which I have put aside, there is a big spiral and several smaller whirls clearly scored, like the signatures of flow currents in a stream. A bored tilemaker? A sudden bubble of creativity? A moment of mutiny? Or a spontaneous expression of sheer joy, not at all like the brisk forefinger sweep of signatures found on Roman tiles. Rather, it makes me think of the long-eared owl deep in the Chauvet cave some 40 miles north of us, its head swivelled right round, traced in a film of clay 36,000 years ago.

23

Taking our Tread

I love the endless variety of our south-facing roof, stretched out like a landscape 'plotted and pieced', as Gerard Manley Hopkins has it in 'Pied Beauty' – 'dappled' and 'brinded' and 'all in stipple'. The faint scent of heated clay, like an earthy oven. The summer surface hot enough to dry fresh figs in a few hours (our neighbour's overhanging fig tree always provides a supply of accidentally dried windfalls). A rolling bluish ocean in moonlight, the frogs calling in the distance for their mates like strange gulls.

Yet an old terracotta roof is made of the ground, as if the ground's clay, baked to hardness, has risen in one piece on its way to the sky, then stopped. Down below, inside, our rooms are spread with its foot-trodden equivalent, clacking where loose. In my study, sheer age has resulted in the *tommette* tiling taking on a gentle swell and dip as centuries-worth of weight sags onto the great beams below, which run across the ceiling of the old goat-house.

In the pre-industrial world, before gigantism on the one hand and nanotechnology on the other, everything artisanal had a similar relation to the human body. Hands massively multiplied and time ignored (whether through

229

communal exaltation or slave labour) led to extraordinary structures like Stonehenge, the Pyramids, Mayan temples, the Pont du Gard with its millimetric precision, or the great Gothic cathedrals – their architect geniuses unnamed. Similarly anonymous people once made many more things themselves, and much more frequently. And mostly better, from baskets to pots. Theirs was an almost unconscious skill, which I witnessed for myself as a teenager in Cameroon, which was then my home: up in the dry and mountainous north where adobe huts cluster like parleys of wizards, our jeep passed a man thatching his own roof from straw, perched naked in the middle as the steep pitch grew up around him.

Such constant closeness to the physical material means that you absorb its qualities. Making jugs from clay scooped nearby, or baskets from local reeds, or platters from wood you have yourself harvested, posits an unbroken flow between origin and creation. When it comes to those diminutive prehistoric scratches on bone, antler, tusk or stone – whether of repeated abstract motifs or, eventually, figurative glimpses of local animals showing an uncanny accuracy of observation (so minimal yet so evocative that you can hear and smell the beast) – we are perhaps at the core of what we now define as art: its distinction from the artisanal melts away. Instead of muddle, order. Instead of confusion, comprehension. An attempt to grasp and hold, not through hunting but through shaping. No elaborate framing, just a direct communication between the maker and the observed. More a conjuring, perhaps.

Was this the original artistic impulse? Both homage and deliberate haunting?

'Everything made by man's hands has a form, which must be either beautiful or ugly,' claimed William Morris, who 'hated' modern civilisation: 'beautiful if it is in accord with Nature, and helps her; ugly if it is discordant with Nature, and thwarts her; it cannot be indifferent.' So the handmade object isn't always lovely; it has to be what we might term *ecologically heedful*. I'm not sure the prehistoric cave paintings of Chauvet, or of Lascaux in the Dordogne, are in any way green, but they show an extraordinary awareness, knowledge and sensitivity of wild things, which may come to much the same. As a boy I was obsessed by the Lascaux paintings, having missed seeing them for real by a fortnight back in the 1960s, when the cave had to be closed to save it from our toxic breath. We bought postcards and I would stare at these over and over again through the ensuing years, marvelling at their realism. Or at how much more 'real' these wild horses or deer or bulls were than anything painted since, including the photographic accuracy of much wildlife imagery. The bristles on the muzzle, the feel of the bony nape, the rolling eyes. I have seen this, the painter seemed to be saying. With my very own eyes. Touched it with my own fingers. This is the underfeeling of it, anyway. In fact, we have no idea whatsoever of what they felt or thought as they dabbed and pressed and stroked in the flamelight. When I showed a postcard of the bison of the far older Chauvet cave to the local woodsman, Claude, still working in the forest in his seventies, he pointed out how well the artist had caught their dainty legs and massive shoulders; Claude had seen them in a reserve on the edge of the Cévennes, and has the sharp visual memory of someone working all day in the woods.

For most of human existence, technology was limb-controlled, dependent on the eye, on breath and effort. I've worked for months at a time in modern factories and assembly lines, and I might as well have been a robot. I think of all hand-built things as rippling out not just from the fingers but from the entire body. Knees, especially. In a Neolithic house near Stonehenge, archaeologists have found knee-prints in the chalk-plaster floor by the hearth: two shallow depressions gradually hollowed out by countless moments tending the fire and cooking. These are not, like our paw-prints, the result of an instant's hazard, but of stubborn application over innumerable years. Sheer abrasion.

In our back cellar, with its medieval fireplace and cobbled floor, there is a stone sink with a circular opening and a space beneath it for a tub. It could be fourteenth century or earlier. The thick stone around the hole is so heavily worn at the front that it has thinned to nothing: the opening is now shaped like a keyhole. In the entrance hall, the sink is larger: a rectangular chunk of limestone chiselled out to a basin no deeper than my thumb, with two further round-edged blocks placed either side, and a drainage hole in one corner. It shows a sunken oval on the right-hand block where countless pots and pans rested as they were scrubbed.

The sole real difference between the Roman dog's paw-print in clay and these shallow, sunken Os in stone is time. Slow the first right down so that the flecks from the impact are all but stilled, and speed the other up to a momentary, ghostly mist of pans and elbows, and you would be watching the same phenomenon. A crater forming, an impression maintained. No deeper than a passing thought. But both, it seems, have endured.

You would have to hang around watching for a lot longer to see another impression forming. This one is on our front-door sill, which consists of a single slab of local *pierre de Pompignan* (a sought-after type of limestone near Pompignan village). It looks at first glance like damage, as if something's gouged or chipped the stone near one corner. Then, after many years of not properly looking, I noticed a corrugation inside, and realised it was a fossil.

Ensuing research revealed it as part of the stem of a crinoid, a starfish-like creature both animal and vegetable, whose fronds would billow gently on the end of this stem anchored to the sea-bed by its holdfast. It preyed on micro-organisms and organic particles. It could move short distances on its long and flexible stalk, which looked like a corrugated drainpipe; it was actually a vertical stack of calcite rings. Our fragment shows a negative of the outside of the stack — an external mould; walking in the garrigue scrub, we often find inside impressions, too, disarmingly obvious on stones scattered over chalky paths through the tangled brush.

The stem itself has dissolved away, leaving the mould. It dates from between 140 and 195 million years ago. This ancientness is as meaningless to our brains as the distances to the stars. I look at the bright spot of Jupiter and its pin-prick moons through my telescope and cannot conceive of the distance – hundreds of millions of miles – between us. But what I can imagine is that whoever first placed this thick slab in front of the door, maybe more than a century ago, had noticed the fossil.

The slab itself bears a strong resemblance to a sandy sea floor, mostly smooth but with tiny worms and coils and bumps in the bluish greyness. In fact, this is the deposit of fine material – countless shells and skeletons of marine creatures falling through the shallow seas – that settled on the dead crinoid and, unstirred by currents or footfall, gently entombed it. A few more million years, assuming no disturbance, and this silt turned into rock.

Reaching the front-door sill means climbing up our external curve of stairs – smooth slabs of the same rock. We are heedless of what dizzying depths of time we press as we mount and descend. The staircase itself may be at least two or three centuries old, so that we have two simultaneous epochs taking our tread, one so shallow in comparison to the other that it can hardly be measured. We have to forget the deeper, or everything drowns – books, family, ideals, kindness, with the list including God, or whatever gods we might believe in. Geological time can be understood intellectually, scientifically, but not spiritually or emotionally. Not literally. And now it takes our footfall, as heedless as ourselves.

24

Epilogue

This year, while finally sealing our chronically leaking second-floor balcony (created, as explained earlier, by the previous owners removing the attic roof where it sloped very low), a builder pulled out a drainpipe and left a hole, prior to spreading the sealant and laying the tiles. It rained overnight: a real Cévenol deluge. Assessing the damage in my study the following day, somewhat flustered, I stepped backwards and knocked over the funerary urn. It landed and rolled briefly but excitedly, scattering black bits over the floor, like the residue of burnt toast or ground coffee; three of the urn's repaired parts lay broken off. Without thinking, I swept the remains of the dead Etruscan into my palm and returned them to the urn. The three sherds fitted back without glue. The storm damage was minimal but upsetting: a treasured photo-portrait of my mother as a young woman, and a large aquatint of Sappho with swans and her two bare-breasted lovers collected long ago by my grandfather (who briefly ran an art gallery in Edwardian London) and which I'd innocently admired all through my childhood. It was particularly upsetting because the study had leaked at one end for as long as we'd been here – a quarter of a century – and this was the last possible opportunity for the rain to surprise. Thanks to the new hole, the drips had fallen in an entirely fresh spot, consistently dry for decades, where I had placed some of what was most valuable to me.

Hubris. Weather is so much to do with the present. Climate is to do with the past and the future. Our mistreatment of the planet will possibly deny us a future, or a meaningful future in terms of civilised conduct and a bearable existence. Right now I'm annoyed with the builder, with my own lapse in not reminding him about the hole, and with the storm itself – which arrived at precisely the wrong time. But storms are heedless of everything, from holes to wedding parties.

And the storms are getting worse, just as our winters have grown milder, the summers hotter and hotter. At time of writing, the autumn is refreshing us with cooler air but bringing no sign of rain. It is October in the Cévennes, and it hasn't rained properly since early June. This is a proper drought. *Désolant*, as a villager put it, a powerful word which includes both 'distressing' and 'appalling'. Stream-beds are dry, plants and trees are parched, and the wild animals along with them. The old Cévenol saying, 'Au mois d'août, sous la pierre, humidité' ('In the month of August, moisture under stones') did not apply this year. I have just returned from a hike on beautiful Mont Aigoual (meaning 'rich in water' in Oc), and the trees' water-stress is not only visible in the withered leafage but palpable in the air. The mountains' famous waterfalls are silent.

It's autumn, but no one is planting in their *potager*, the soil is too dry and friable. Our view shows brown stains like tea on the hills' drapery of scrub oak. Oddly, the village drinking fountains have gone on trickling throughout, and the great fountains of Nîmes still gush into the sunlight. Things are slightly better deep underground, after a wet spring, but the situation is *préoccupant*, as the meteorologists tactfully put it, who can only read and analyse the signs and have no power to solve anything. Scientists' predictions are not reassuring: in a few decades, or even less, Languedoc will have a Moroccan climate, with the vegetation and animals to go with it.

If nothing is done, and the dishonesty, stupidity and plain ignorance of certain of the world's most powerful leaders and industrialists continue to hold sway over common sense and the underlying innovative brilliance of humankind, then this book will turn out to have been not so much a memoir as a memorial. Climate change is as the Black Death was in the fourteenth century: it respects no borders, travels shockingly fast and touches every class of person – most especially the poor. A plague is temporary; climate change will spread on into the future, touching generations to come. Perhaps when civilisation breaks down under its pressure, the oceans will restock and cool, the forests spread, the ice reform, the wild creatures multiply. But such panoptic, biblical predictions are hard to feel good about. We work on much smaller, domestic, personal scales. Calamity is only meaningful to us when it rips off our roof, reduces our vegetable patch to a dustbowl, sends us running from the waters, drowns our streets and fields.

I like the fact that, in the hardened ash of that Tanzanian site at Laetoli, there are impressions of raindrops. They look like dents alongside the traces of countless animals – including the upright hominids, who may have lifted their faces to catch the cooling water on their tongues.

Ephemerality and permanence.

Except that, by all accounts, the ash-rock itself is now as fragile as a biscuit, and has been hidden again under earth, like all memories.

FOOTPRINTS

for Sacha

We're walking over the highest hills of France,
my son on my shoulders, and he's on to footprints now,
the prints of boots and dogs in the path's slough
between the stunted pines and heather and flung grass.

He wants to know where ours are. 'Ours are behind.'
'Why aren't our footprints there in front?' 'Because
we're not there yet. Footprints come out from us.'
'Footprints aren't ever where you haven't been'd?'

'No.' My wife carries our seven-week-old daughter
in a sling. He wants to see his sister make some.
'She's much too young.' 'She'll make them soon!'
'You're aching my shoulders – make some now instead
of later.'

He says 'Oh yes' and I let him down. He runs
ahead, then turns and looks. Beyond is already
what has and has not been : the light fading,
the wind that over the hill-tops sweeps this rain.

ACKNOWLEDGEMENTS

It would be impossible to thank personally all those who have, over the last twenty-seven years, contributed to this book (whether knowingly or not), but I am deeply grateful for their help, generosity and, in many cases, friendship. Most names have been changed out of respect to the living as well as the dead.

A special thanks to Bill Homewood and Estelle Kohler for their invaluable counsel, to Stephen Marsden for the moulds and to Michelle Jolly for the sherds and stories. Thank you to André Mourizard for the swingle tree and to David Crackanthorpe for guidance on the Camisard rebellion. I am grateful to the Houix family for their help in the early days and in particular to the late Sébastien Houix.

Many of these chapters started life as a 'Freelance' column in the *Times Literary Supplement*, where they were superbly edited by James Campbell. Subsequently, Jamie Birkett at Bloomsbury Continuum suggested that I adapt and add to them for a book, happily under his equally fine editorship. Thank you to both and to my agent Lucy Luck for accompanying the transition, and to Neil Gower for the illustrations.

Once again, my wife Jo made crucial suggestions and generally jogged my faulty memory, as well as managing our lives here in true Cévenol fashion. Thank you also to my children, Josh, Sacha and Anna (a Nîmoise by birth), for going along with their parents' whim and accepting to be nurtured by the southern hills without complaint.

Among the numerous books I have consulted over the years, I owe a particular debt to the beautiful if hefty second volume (*Les activités agricoles*) of *Le temps cévenol, la conscience d'une terre*, by Jean-Noël Pelen and Daniel Travier (Sedilan, 1984), edited and printed locally and now classified as rare. Although I first read it several years after beginning my own 'notes', Geoffrey Grigson's *Notes from an Odd Country* (Macmillan, 1970) proved a quiet inspiration.

Adam Thorpe was born in Paris and brought up in India, Cameroon and England. His first collection of poetry was published in 1988 and was shortlisted for the Whitbread Poetry Award. His first novel, *Ulverton*, was published to critical acclaim in 1992 and is now a Vintage Classic. He has since published ten novels, seven collections of poetry, two works of non-fiction and two books of short stories, as well as writing numerous radio plays. His first work of non-fiction, *On Silbury Hill*, was BBC Radio 4's Book of the Week. He has also published new translations of Flaubert's *Madame Bovary* and Zola's *Thérèse Raquin*. His latest novel, *Missing Fay*, was a *Guardian* and a *Sunday Times* Book of the Year in 2017. He has lived in France with his family since 1990.

A NOTE ON THE TYPE

The text of this book is set in Fournier. Fournier is derived from the *romain du roi*, which was created towards the end of the seventeenth century from designs made by a committee of the Académie of Sciences for the exclusive use of the Imprimerie Royale. The original Fournier types were cut by the famous Paris founder Pierre Simon Fournier in about 1742. These types were some of the most influential designs of the eight and are counted among the earliest examples of the 'transitional' style of typeface. This Monotype version dates from 1924. Fournier is a light, clear face whose distinctive features are capital letters that are quite tall and bold in relation to the lower-case letters, and *decorative italics, which show the influence of the calligraphy of Fournier's time.*